Use It! Don't Lose It!

LANGUAGE
Daily Skills Practice
Grade 7

by Marjorie Frank

IncentivePublications

Thanks to Erin Linton
for her assistance in researching topics,
checking facts, and tracking down trivia.

Illustrated by Kathleen Bullock
Cover by Geoffrey Brittingham
Edited by Jill Norris
Copy-edited by Cary Grayson

ISBN 978-0-86530-652-3

4   5   6   7   8   9   10   09

Printed by Sheridan Books, Inc., Chelsea, Michigan • November 2009
www.incentivepublications.com

Don't let those language skills get lost or rusty!

As a teacher you work hard to teach language skills to your students. Your students work hard to master them. Do you worry that your students will forget the material as you move on to the next concept?

If so, here's a plan for you and your students—one that will keep those skills sharp.

Use It! Don't Lose It! provides daily language practice for all the basic skills. There are five language problems a day, every day for 36 weeks. The skills are correlated to national and state standards.

Students practice all the seventh grade skills, concepts, and processes in a spiraling sequence. The plan starts with the simplest level of seventh grade skills, progressing gradually to higher-level tasks, as it continually circles around and back to the the same skills at a little higher level, again and again. Each time a skill shows up, it has a new context—requiring students to dig into their memories, recall what they know, and apply it to another situation.

The Weekly Plan—Five Problems a Day for 36 Weeks

Monday – Thursday .... • one vocabulary or other word skills item
• one spelling or mechanics item (capitalization, punctuation)
• one grammar or language usage item

Monday and Wednesday .... • one reading item
• one literature item

Tuesday and Thursday .... • one writing item
• one research/information skills item

Friday .... • one longer reading comprehension passage with questions
• one writing task

Contents

How to Use Daily Skills Practice

To get started, reproduce each page, slice the Monday–Thursday lesson pages in half or prepare a transparency. The lessons can be used . . .

- **for independent practice**—Reproduce the lessons and let students work individually or in pairs to practice skills at the beginning or end of a language class.

- **for small group work**—Students can discuss and solve the problems together and agree on answers.

- **for the whole class review**—Make a transparency and work through the problems together as a class.

Helpful Hints for Getting Started

- Though students may work alone on the items, always find a way to review and discuss the answers together. In each review, ask students to describe how they solved the problem-solving problems or other problems that involve choices of strategies.

- Allow more time for the Friday lesson, as these tasks may take a little longer. Students can work in small groups to discover and discuss their answers.

- Provide dictionaries and other resources that may be helpful to students as needed. There will not always be room on the sheet for some of the longer writing tasks.

- Many of the writing tasks can be expanded into full writing lessons. When you have time to do so, extend the activity to work on all or various stages of the writing process. Find time for students to share and enjoy their written products.

- The daily lessons are designed to be completed in a short time period, so that they can be used along with your regular daily instruction. However, don't end the discussion until you are sure all students "get it," or at least until you know which ones don't get something and will need extra instruction. This will strengthen all the other work students do in language class.

- Keep a consistent focus on thinking skills for reading comprehension activities. Allow students to discuss their answers, particularly those that involve higher level thinking skills such as drawing conclusions, inferring, predicting, or evaluating.

- Find ways to strengthen the knowledge and use of new vocabulary words students learn in the daily practice. Keep a running list of these words. Use them in classroom discussions and activities. Find ways to share and show off knowledge of the words. Encourage students to include the new words in their writing.

- Take note of which items leave some or all of the students confused or uncertain. This will alert you to which skills need more instruction.

- The daily lessons may include some topics or skills your students have not yet learned. In these cases, students may skip items. Or, you might encourage them to consider how the problem could be solved. Or, you might use the occasion for a short lesson that would get them started on this skill.

1. Edit the sentence.

legends say that the great sea monster, the kraken, attacked a ship named the marie celeste off the scandanavian coast.

2. Circle the prefixes that mean **not**.

contrary   improper   inedible   displace

nonstop   antibiotic   unclear   illegible

3. Change this into a complete sentence.

The Kraken, having long slimy tentacles.

4. The Kraken is a legendary sea creature. What is the genre (kind) of this description?

> Below the thunders of the upper sea;
> Far, far beneath in the abysmal deep
> About his shadowy sides
>   the faintest sunlights flee
> The Kraken lies in ancient, dreamless sleep.

5. Which statements are opinions?

   a. John Wyndham wrote a novel called **The Kraken Wakes.**

   b. It is not possible for a sea creature to sink a ship.

   c. Nothing has frightened any sailor as much as the Kraken.

   d. Supposedly, the Kraken lives in the cold waters near Scandinavia.

Ooooh, I'm scared!

MONSTERS of the DEEP

1. Add the correct ending punctuation.

Keep your eyes open for mermaids

2. An outline of information (contained in a book), listed in the order that the information occurs, is

   ○ a bibliography   ○ a table of contents

   ○ an index   ○ a preface

3. Circle the complete subject.

Mythical creatures, such as mermaids and mermen, are often found in art and literature.

4. Would it be accurate to refer to mermaids as **elusive**?

5. Cross out the unnecessary words.

According to popular beliefs, it is thought that mermaids are half human and half fish, made up of two different animals. The legends describe beautiful, singing creatures that attracted the attention of passing sailors sailing by, so the stories say. The sailors would become distracted by the mermaids, the distractions causing their ships to crash on the rocks.

1. Identify the rhyme pattern in the poem.

   Mermaids sit upon the rocks
   And comb their golden hair.
   Sailors listen, stop, and stare,
   But are the mermaids really there?

2. Circle the correctly spelled words.

   acheive   piece   weigh   hieght   either

3. What is the meaning of the bold word?

   Joe was hurt by his friends' laughter and teasing as they **derided** him about his belief in Bigfoot.

4. Which sentences are correct?

   a. Are you the one who saw Bigfoot?

   b. To who did you give those pictures?

   c. Whoever believes in Bigfoot, raise your hand.

5. Circle the sentence that is out of sequence.

   In 1947, John Green began his career as a newsreporter. At that time, he thought the Bigfoot sightings were just tall tales. By 2001, he had gathered over 4,000 reports of incidents involving some large creature. However, over the next ten years, many people he respected had claimed to see the creature. Then, in late 1958, he saw casts of 16-inch footprints for himself. That inspired him to investigate Bigfoot sightings. All his research led him to take the claims about Bigfoot much more seriously.

1. What part of speech is the underlined word?

   After a recent <u>climb</u> in the Himalayas, Amalie insisted that she had confronted a Yeti.

2. Choose the most precise word.

   Climbers were _____ by deep, huge footprints that crossed the trail.

   interested   startled   alerted   threatened

3. Number the words in alphabetical order.

   ___ Bigfoot   ___ bifocal   ___ bighearted

   ___ biennial   ___ bijou   ___ beggar

4. Circle the synonyms for **incredulous**.

   dubious   ludicrous

   doubtful   suspicious

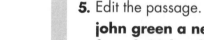

5. Edit the passage.

   john green a newspaper reporter from british columbia followed stories of the sasquatch for almost fifty years he believes that the existence of the sasquatch has never been proved however he points out two things that have been proved the existence of some huge deep footprints and the thousands of credible people who claim to have seen a large hairy bipedal creature

Name

Read

1. What is the main idea of the poem?

2. To which sense does the poem appeal most strongly?

3. Circle two examples of repetition.

4. What nouns are used to name the famous Nessie?

5. Reread the phrases that have helped you form a picture of Nessie. Draw that picture.

Did you hear anything?

Beneath the murky waters
Of Loch Ness, dark and cold
Lurks one mysterious monster—
A legend, centuries old.

It's said that Nessie's mouth is wide,
Her neck is long and slim.
She lifts her head and stretches tall
When she rises for a swim.

That long, white body, snake-like neck
And broad, imposing head
Spark curiosity and thrill in some—
In others, fear and dread.

Some claim she isn't there at all,
That the creature isn't real,
That sightings are of fish or waves,
A mirage, or possibly a seal.

But what about the video?
Some stealthy serpent in the lake,
Ten feet long with dancing head—
Proof on film, or just a fake?

Thousands seek to see her.
Thousands more will try.
She's ever so elusive
Hiding, maybe shy.

She's Scotland's favorite monster,
And tourists stalk her, too.
I'm on my way to search because
I believe she's there; do you?
I believe she's there; do you?

Write

1. Write a summary of the poem.

2. Give the poem a good title.

1. Circle the proper nouns.

iceberg   the Titanic

St. John's Glacier   Bering Sea

melting glaciers   ice cream

2. Put commas where they are needed.

For most icebergs such as the one that was hit by the Titanic nine-tenths of the mass is below the surface of the water.

3. Which words are not compounds?

○ iceberg   ○ frostbite   ○ shipwreck   ○ sinkable

○ icicle   ○ defrost   ○ snowshoes   ○ submerge

4. From this passage, can you tell how icebergs are formed?

The icebergs in the North Atlantic Ocean mostly come from glaciers along the coast of Greenland. The icebergs last about a year before melting.

5. What can you tell about the attitude or bias of the sign's writer?

Will there be hot chocolate?

Welcome to Lacey Glacier

Notice the beautiful colors!
Feel the ice!
Walk, relax, sit, or slide on the glacier!
Appreciate the fact that this glacier took many years to form!
Keep your visit fun and safe.
Pay attention to all signs.

Enjoy your visit!

Summer hours 8 am –7 pm

1. Which is the denotation of the word **iceberg**?

a. massive ice floe that mostly hides beneath the water and causes shipwrecks

b. large floating mass of ice detached from a glacier

2. Circle the correctly spelled words.

apologise   **criticize**   **surprize**

televise   **realise**   **exercize**

3. Name five third person pronouns.

4. The word glacial would be found on page _____.

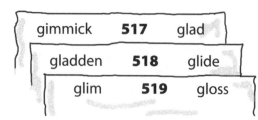

gimmick	**517**	glad
gladden	**518**	glide
glim	**519**	gloss

5. Which are examples of descriptive writing?

a. brochure advertising glacier trips

b. essay on reasons for receding glaciers

c. poem about beautiful glacial colors

d. tale about a talking iceberg

e. explanation of the size, shape, weight, and location of a giant iceberg

See the Antarctic Glaciers

Just reading about these things makes me cold.

1. Which is the simple sentence?

    a. Unlike most glaciers, the Bering Glacier moves quickly.

    b. The glacier advances 300 feet a year.

    c. Is it true that icebergs come from glaciers?

2. Circle the antonym for **deception**.

    duplicity   obligation   fraud   candor

3. Capitalize the book title correctly.

    the day the titanic sank

4. Circle the cause. Underline the effect.

    Snow falls and stays on the ground all year long. Eventually it packs down, hardens, and forms glaciers.

5. What is the author's purpose for writing this?

    The end of a glacier is a snout. The ice is melting quickly at the glacier's snout. If the glacier ends at a body of water, the snout breaks off into icebergs. Some of these icebergs are as big as small countries.

What are you doing here?

I'm waiting for the next Ice Age.

1. Give three different meanings for the word **seal**.

2. Correct the misspelled words.

    meny   wether   aumze

    emty   histery   cought

    people   benefit   glacier

3. Which sentences are correct?

    a. Him and I visited the glacier.

    b. Did you and she see the icebergs?

    c. Pass the dry ice to Max and I.

    d. Is that picture for me?

4. Get ready to write a paragraph telling why you would (or would not) like to float on an iceberg. Write a topic sentence for this paragraph.

5. Examine the picture. Predict what will happen next.

Uh, oh!

CRACK!   SNAP!

Name

Read

1. What is **till**?

2. How do glacial lakes form?

3. Make an inference about what **meltwater** is.

4. Abrading is the scraping and scouring of the rock surface that happens as a glacier moves over it. From the information in the diagram, draw a conclusion about the material that actually does the abrading.

5. What is the difference between **outwash** and a **moraine**?

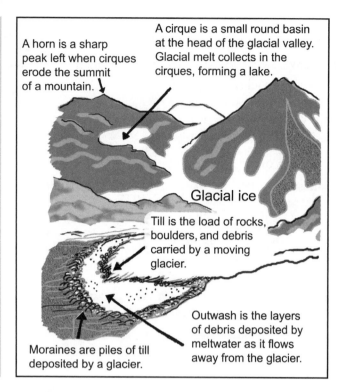

A horn is a sharp peak left when cirques erode the summit of a mountain.

A cirque is a small round basin at the head of the glacial valley. Glacial melt collects in the cirques, forming a lake.

Glacial ice

Till is the load of rocks, boulders, and debris carried by a moving glacier.

Outwash is the layers of debris deposited by meltwater as it flows away from the glacier.

Moraines are piles of till deposited by a glacier.

They called it "unsinkable" but the *titanic* was not they called it a floating luxury hotel and indeed it was! it was like a grand palace with huge rooms gold-plated light fixtures a swimming pool and steam baths. no ship this big or beautiful had ever been built before hundreds of passengers boarded the *titanic* in Southampton England on April 10 1912. The great new Ship was bound for new york on its maiden voyage.

At a half hour past midnight on April 15 1912 disaster struck the *titanic* actually the ship struck disaster in the form of an iceberg. At first passengers didnt realize that the accident was serious there was a command for people to get into the lifeboats. Unfortunately the company that built the boat was so convinced it was unsinkable that they had sent lifeboats for only about half of the people on board.

The ship sent out distress signals hoping nearby ships would come to help the bow of the *titanic* was sinking when a loud roaring noise went up from the ship. the *titanic* was breaking apart it stood up in the air for a short time soon to disappear beneath the waves. The next day another ship the *Carpathia* came to rescue 712 survivors. hundreds more did not survive.

There are many theories about why the *titanic* sank seventy-five years later after much searching the ships wreckage was found. small submarines have explored the wreckage. Maybe some of the mysteries of this disaster will now be solved.

Write

1. Edit the passage for punctuation, capitalization, and spelling.

2. Give the passage a good title.

I always wear my life jacket when I go on "unsinkable" ships.

1. A news story begins like this:

   Imagine the strength it would take to pull a large airplane! On October 15, 1997, one man did just that. He set a record by pulling a 200-ton Boeing 747 plane almost three hundred feet.

   What is the point of view of this story?

2. Is the apostrophe used correctly?

   Zhuo Li's weightlifting record was set in 2003.

3. Which word means the **act of competing**?

   ○ competition   ○ competitor   ○ competed

4. Circle the correct word.

   Athletes at the Newtown Bodybuilding Competition (lift, lifts) about 110 kg each.

Weight lifting is an uplifting experience.

Olympic-style weightlifters are some of the strongest men and women in the world. They may not have the biggest muscles, but they do have the strongest, most powerful muscles. Bodybuilders, on the other hand, work for bulk because the emphasis in their sport is the appearance of the muscles. Thus, bodybuilders do not have to be as strong as weightlifters.

5. Does the author have enough information to draw the conclusion written in the last sentence?

1. Rewrite the sentence to show more action.

   With a lift of 300 kg, Ding Meiyian became a women's world champion weightlifter.

2. A powerful weightlifter is sure she can set a new world record today. Is she **confident** or **confidant**?

3. Which key word would be best to use in an encyclopedia search for Olympic weightlifting?

   ○ sports   ○ weights
   ○ weightlifting   ○ Olympics

4. Correct the spelling of these words.

   neumonia   whizard   phisics

   shurely   corus   gastly

5. Correct the usage errors.

   a. **Where are my new weights at?**

   b. **Beside winning today, she won the competition last week.**

   c. **Has he risen the weights above his head?**

   d. **She left her weights laying in the middle of the gym floor.**

   e. **Leave me lift this weight by myself.**

Sometimes I feel weighted down.

1. What is the meaning of this sentence?

Alex bit off more than he could chew by trying to lift 35 kg.

2. Insert the correct punctuation.

These are the weights she lifted in today's practice 84 kg 66.5 kg and 91 kg.

3. Write a possessive phrase meaning *the muscles of a bodybuilder*.

4. To which sense does this description appeal most strongly?

Across the gym, muscles strained and burned. Bodies heated up. Sweat bathed every forehead and trickled down backs to soak into shirts.

5. Lucy got these books at the library. Examine the titles. What can you infer about Lucy's interests?

Amazing Feats of Strength

Building Inner Strength

From Mr. Atlas to Mr. Governor

HOW TO BUILD MUSCLES IN 10 WEEKS

Strength Without Weightlifting

The Woman Who Lifted Trains

1. Write the plural of each word.

donkey   O'Malley   arch   volcano

piano   country   calf   goose

2. Which word does not belong?

○ weighty   ○ strongman

○ courageous   ○ athletic

○ likely   ○ worrisome

3. Circle the past tense verbs.

defeated   bring   win   caught   raised

4. Which reference source is a yearly publication that gives up-to-date information, basic facts, and statistics on many topics?

a. almanac   c. dictionary   e. atlas

b. thesaurus   d. gazetteer   f. encyclopedia

5. Edit the passage.

weightlifting has been around for hundreds of years dating back to ancient greece and egypt? It was featured in the first modern olympic games in athens grease in 1896 in march 1891 the first world weightlifting championships were held in londen england. the international weightlifting federation was founded in 1905 currently over 160 countries participate in the organisation

Name

Ta, da!

Read

1. Identify the form of writing (i.e., poem, article, story, etc.) for each example.
2. What is the main idea of example a?
3. Which example is imaginative?
4. Which examples are expository?
5. Which weightlifting event is composed of two motions?

a.

_____

There are two events in Olympic-style weightlifting competitions. The winner in any competition is the athlete who lifts the highest amount of weight in the combined weights of two lifts. In the snatch, the bar (with weights) is lifted from the ground to full arms overhead in one continuous motion. The clean and jerk is two motions. The barbell is lifted from the floor to the shoulders in one continuous motion (the clean), then from the shoulders to overhead in a second continuous motion (the jerk).

b.

Bruno: Why did the bodybuilder get fired from his job at the gas station?

Buster: Because he kept pumping iron instead of gas.

c.

_____

Arnold Schwarzenegger is probably the most famous bodybuilder of all time. Born in Austria in 1947, he gained notoriety with his seven wins of the "Mr. Olympia" title from 1970 to 1980. He was nicknamed "The Austrian Oak." Arnold's movie career began in 1970 with Hercules in New York. As an actor, he is best known for the Terminator movies. In 2003, he exchanged the "Terminator" title for the title of "Governor," when he was elected governor of California.

d.

_____

A snatch is a snap for Lulu Beasy
She's great at the clean and jerk.
She makes these feats look really easy.
But they're quite a lot of work.
She lifted 60 pounds today.
Half her body weight or so
To victory she was on her way
Till _____

Write

1. Write titles for examples a, c, and d.
2. Write the final line for example d.
3. Write three questions you would like to ask Arnold Schwarzenegger.

e. **Used Weights Wanted —** Will buy free weights in good condition—10, 12, 15, 25, 50 pounds. Call Jojo, 555-9909 or email jojob@bubba.net

1. As the morning of November 22, dawned, Blackbeard the Pirate had no idea what fate would befall him before the day ended.

The passage above is an example of

a. onomatopoeia   c. irony

b. personification   d. foreshadowing

2. Circle the objective pronouns.

We told them the story of Anne Bonny, the female pirate. Everyone wanted to hear more about her.

3. Write the past tense of each verb.

capture   escape   worry
catch   rob   fight

Avast, me hearties.

4. Is it logical that the word **depraved** might be associated with pirates?

5. Write a summary of this passage.

Piracy is the crime of robbery or other violent acts, committed for private reasons, on the high seas. People who commit such acts are called *pirates.* They attack and loot ships of any nation or private ownership. *Privateers* commit robbery also, but for slightly different reasons. These looters operate with permission and direction of a particular nation, to represent them during wartime and to attack certain ships in certain areas. A group of 17th century privateers called themselves *buccaneers.* They became wealthy robbing Spanish ships.

Whatever the specific name of the seafarers, these characters committed much violence and devastation at sea.

1. Write the plural of each noun.

buccaneer   treasure   radio   match
tomato   bounty   child   bath

2. Is the statement true or false?

A biography of pirate Mary Read would be found in the library in a section where books are alphabetized by the last names of the authors.

3. Add correct punctuation.

Aarrr growled Captain Jack gimme yer loot or ye'll walk the plank

4. What is the meaning of the underlined word?

Pirates often <u>plundered</u> ships, leaving nothing of value behind.

5. Write a caption for the picture.

Gulp!

1. What is the main idea?

It was fitting that Blackbeard died a violent death. This vicious man wreaked devastation and death on over 40 ships in his career. He carried swords, pistols, and knives at all times. With his harsh temper and scary black beard, he terrorized everyone, including his own crew. He was a nasty, fearsome man.

2. Circle the words that need capital letters.

even though flags differed from ship to ship, the name jolly roger is given to all pirate flags.

3. Identify the sentence as declarative, imperative, exclamatory, or interrogative.

Ahoy, Mateys, how're ye doin' today?

4. What is the tone of the passage in question one?

Well, shiver me timbers.

X marks the spot.

5. Replace each incorrect homonym.

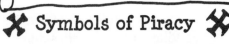

✗ Symbols of Piracy ✗

parrots — The site of a parrot sitting near Long John Silver's caller came from the Treasure Island story.

peg legs — This symbol came from Treasure Island, two. Pirates mite knead to have injured legs cut off to ease pane and save there lives.

hooks — This cymbal began with Captain Hook in the Peter Pan story. It is true, a pirate might lose a hand in battle. A blacksmith maid a hook from medal found on bored the ship.

the plank — The symbol brings too mind enemies cent to walk a plank into the see.

1. Write two or three sentences describing a pirate's flag that you would design. Include specific details. Then draw the flag.

2. Circle the conjunction.

An 1856 declaration outlawed privateering, but it was not honored by all countries.

3. Correct the spelling.

echoe   volcanoe   mosquitos

altoes   prontoe   mottoes

4. Finish the analogy.

Blackbeard : piracy :: _____ : entertainment

_____

5. Alphabetize these movies.

DVD Sale

The Princess Bride

Wolves of the Sea

The Curse of the Sea

Treasure Island

The Adventures of Peter Pan

The Pirate's Daughter

Pirates of the Caribbean

Read

1. Find the treasure spot on the map. Mark it with an X.

Go five miles due south from Peg Leg Ville; head two miles due west, then four miles northeast, then two miles west.

2. What is the elevation difference between Peg Leg Ville and the spot where the X is marked?

3. What map location is southeast of Peg Leg Ville?

4. How much higher (elevation) is Spy Peak than the treasure location?

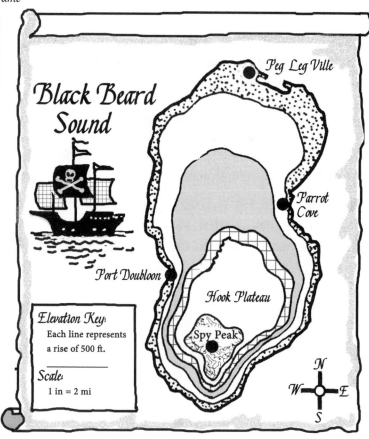

Black Beard Sound

Peg Leg Ville

Parrot Cove

Port Doubloon

Hook Plateau

Spy Peak

Elevation Key:
Each line represents a rise of 500 ft.

Scale:
1 in = 2 mi

Some Pirate Vocabulary

ahoy – hello

arrr! – exclamation

aye – yes

aye, aye – agreement

avast – attention, hey, wow

beauty – woman

belay – give, transfer, pass

bilge rat – humorous insult to friends

bow – front of ship

briny deep – salty sea

cap'n – captain

cutlass – pirate sword

Davy Jones' Locker – bottom of the ocean

disembark – get off the ship

embark – get on the ship

grog – pirate drink

hornpipe – pirate dance

Jolly Roger – flag

keelhaul – a punishment

landlubber – land lover

matey – friend

me – my, mine

me hearties – my friends

mutiny – turn or conspire against the captain

ne'er-do-well – scoundrel

pieces of eight – Spanish silver coins

plunder – rob

port – left side of ship

rigging – ropes that hold the sails in place

spyglass – telescope

starboard – right side of ship

stern – back of ship

wastrel – useless person

weigh anchor – get ready to leave

ye – you, your, yours

y'er – your

yardarm – pole extended from mast to support a square sail; also used to hang enemies.

Write

Write a conversation between two pirates, or a speech a pirate might give to another pirate or group of pirates. Use as much of the pirate vocabulary as you can.

It's the pirate's life for me.

1. Circle examples with correct hyphen use.

motor-cycle	**one-third**	**speed-way**
ex-boyfriend	**time-out**	**sister-in-law**

2. Which word does not belong?

rescind   recite   revoke   repeal

3. Which is an example of imaginative writing?

    a. an article about motorcycle racing

    b. a novel about a soapbox derby champion

    c. an essay on concerns about the safety of lawnmower racing

    d. the biography of a Daytona 500 winner

4. Is this statement fact or opinion?

Off-road racing is the most dangerous and difficult of all motor racing sports.

5. Write the missing verb tenses.

present – **speed**	present – **take**
past –	past –
future –	future –

present – **choose**	present – **cheer**
past –	past –
future –	future –

present – **lie**	present – **win**
past –	past –
future –	future –

I run with a fast crowd.

1. Sue's race time was 85 seconds better than she had hoped. Did this performance **accede** or **exceed** her expectations?

2. Give the comparative and superlative forms of the adverb **dangerously**.

3. One word shows up twice. Explain both meanings of the word.

Cici can sit on my lap to watch the last lap of the race.

4. Cross out words that are not needed.

To qualify for a soap box derby, your age must be 9–16 years old. Also, you must build your car yourself, besides that.

I may be homemade – but I can fly.

5. Tell two things someone could learn by reading this encyclopedia entry.

The Baja 1000 is a well-known 1000-mile off-road race. In off-road racing, different kinds of vehicles compete in races over terrain that is not on a regular paved track. Like the Baja 1000, many of these races take place in the desert, but off-road racing has expanded to cover different kinds of environments such as hilly routes. There are also several different classes of vehicles, including cars. Vehicles must withstand miles of rough travel.

1. What words or phrases create sensory appeal?

Shrill shrieks, sudden cheers, and ooohs from the crowd accompanied tire screeches and engine growls.

2. Give an antonym for the word **stationary**.

3. Choose the correct word.

The off-road racing organization (**plan, plans**) about six major races a year.

4. Edit the heading and greeting of this letter.

beaseley's race car repair shop
6400 whitewater way
franklin tn 37064
april 13 2006

dear mrs lasley

I can fix that!

5. What did Julie do just before she started on her soapbox car design?

Julie ordered the rules for the soapbox derby. While she waited for them to come, she found some books and websites about the derby. She also signed up for a soapbox building class. When the rules came, Julie studied the section about the stock division. She found someone to help her build the car and started creating a design. When she figured out how complicated this would be, she decided to order a kit for making the car.

1. Use each word as a part of two different compound words. Make it the beginning of one word and the ending of another.

side   off   down   out

2. Which example is correct?

a. Who was it that won that race?

b. Give the trophy to whoever won the race.

I'm here for the Derby.

3. Circle the correctly spelled words.

holyness   solidifying   worrysome

penniless   ladilike   petrified

4. Which cannot be found in a dictionary?

a. world records   c. word meanings

b. word pronunciations   d. synonyms

5. What mood is set by this selection?

The crowd is buzzing with anticipation. Excited young competitors tingle as they arrive in Akron, Ohio, from all over the world. This is it—the big race they have worked so hard for—the All-American Soapbox Derby! A full police escort welcomes each competitor. The band plays as they arrive, and cheers go up as the names are announced. Wow—a personal introduction to the whole crowd! And then, the big thrill comes as the racers are introduced to Derby Downs—the track where they will race.

Name

Read

1. What kind of car was driven by a winner from Columbia?
2. What is the difference between the 1987 and 1986 speeds?
3. What is noticeable about the 1984 and 1991 wins?
4. What percent of the winning cars are not March-Cosworths?
5. What is the purpose of this table?
6. Draw one conclusion from this information.

On your mark,
Get set, ...

10 FASTEST WINNING SPEEDS AT THE INDIANAPOLIS 500 AUTO RACE

	DRIVER	COUNTRY	SPEED MPH	YEAR	CAR MAKE
1	Arie Luyendyk	Netherlands	185.981	1990	Lola-Chevrolet
2	Rick Mears	U.S.A.	176.457	1991	Chevrolet-Lumina
3	Bobby Rahal	U.S.A.	170.722	1986	March-Cosworth
4	Juna Pablo Montoya	Columbia	167.607	2000	G Force-Aurora
5	Emerson Fittipaldi	Brazil	167.581	1989	Penske-Chevrolet
6	Helio Castroneves	Brazil	166.499	2002	Dallara-Chevrolet
7	Rick Mears	U.S.A.	163.612	1984	March-Cosworth
8	Mark Donohue	U.S.A.	162.962	1972	McLaren-Offenhauser
9	Al Unser	U.S.A.	162.175	1987	March-Cosworth
10	Tom Sneva	U.S.A.	162.117	1983	March-Cosworth

Write

Finish the comparisons.

1. Her soapbox reminds me of a_____
2. The race was as noisy as_____
3. The crowd sounded like _____
4. Before the race, my stomach felt like _____
5. Racing motorcycles are as _____ as _____
6. His car was faster than_____
7. Going to a soapbox derby could be more fun than _____

MONDAY WEEK 6 _____ LANGUAGE PRACTICE
Name

1. What is the meaning of the underlined word?

   The smell of the <u>nectar</u> attracts insects to the sundew plant. Once they land, they are trapped—stuck in that sweet substance.

2. Which examples contain linking verbs?

   a. A Venus flytrap has a set of jaws.

   b. The bladderwort is a meat-eating plant.

   c. The plant snapped shut, trapping the fly.

   d. Pitcher plants trap insects in slippery cups.

3. Circle the correctly spelled words.

cancel	bundle	gargel
wrestel	terrible	visibal

4. What literary technique is used in this example?

   "Time for lunch," mused the clever bladderwort as he lazed about the pond. With that thought, he made a plan to get his trap doors ready.

5. Where does the Saguaro cactus store water?

I feel a little bloated.

   Many cactus plants thrive in dry climates by serving as storage tanks for water. When it does rain in the desert, the Saguaro takes in water and holds it in an expandable stem. A large Saguaro cactus can hold several tons of water.

TUESDAY WEEK 6 _____ LANGUAGE PRACTICE
Name

1. Is the punctuation correct?

   Here are some ways that dolphins communicate: by growling, moaning, whistling, and squeaking.

2. Underline the indirect object.

   Mud puddles give pigs a place to cool off.

3. Circle the correct word.

   A fuzzy caterpillar might make a good pet (accept, except) for the poisonous, stinging spires that can irritate your skin.

4. Write a topic sentence for a paragraph about how the length of a giraffe's neck affects its life and activities.

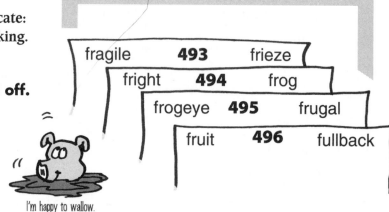

I'm happy to wallow.

fragile	493	frieze
fright	494	frog
frogeye	495	frugal
fruit	496	fullback

5. Write the dictionary page number on which each word would be found.

   a. frozen _____   d. fuel _____

   b. frogman _____   e. fritter _____

   c. friction _____   f. fresco _____

1. What is the meaning of the word **quadriped**?

2. Circle the cause. Underline the effect.

The coating a pig gets from rolling around in mud protects her from nasty insect bites and sunburn.

3. Rewrite this sentence correctly.

If you're a bug, don't never go near a Venus flytrap plant.

4. Edit the sentence.

Sarah, how is it that tree frog able to climb up the window without sliding down asked Sam

I got my tongue caught in a Venus' Flytrap.

5. Identify one or more effective writing techniques used by the author.

"Roar!" "Huff!" "Whoosh!" The lion noisily stands and shake outs his mighty mane. Like a huge shield, the mane challenges the other lions. Its hairy bristles and massive size trumpet this warning: "I am strong and powerful. Stay away from me and my territory."

1. Which means a **contradictory statement**?

○ query   ○ paradox
○ paraphrase   ○ conundrum

2. Write a word that contains a silent letter for each of these definitions.

crypt   a sacred song

chew with the teeth   stem of a plant

3. What information can be found on the spine of a book?

4. Circle any prepositions. Draw a box around any objects of prepositions.

The shaggy mane protects the lion's neck during fights with other lions.

My car got 'toad'.

That's a frog joke.

5. Rewrite each sentence with an active verb.

a. I am fascinated by that frog!

b. The tree frog's position on the window is precarious.

c. It appears that the fingers and toes are sticky.

d. Three frogs are on the window now.

e. The frog on the sunny window seems sleepy.

Read

1. Give the animal's name that is used as the basis for each beast.
2. What is the purpose of these selections?
3. Which example describes the fewest different body parts of the beast?
4. Use the information in the descriptions to draw three of the beasts.

Backward Beasts are wonderful imaginary monsters. To create one:
- Think of a common animal.
- Write its name backwards.
- Turn on your imagination and picture the new creature.

Call me Licnep, please.

Backward Beasts

The grumpy TAR has 18 feet
And only dines on roasted meat.
With two big fangs he's terribly fat!
But turned around, he's a little _____.

Long whiskers grow on a LIAUQ's face,
She's got red scales all over the place—
On her skinny neck and her powerful tail.
But turned around, she's a chubby _____.

The TARROP has such awful teeth
Three up above, and six beneath.
Turn him around, give him a carrot.
He's just a friendly, chatty _____.

The wings and claws upon a WOC
Are hard and scratchy as a rock.
The squarish snout spouts fire, but now . . .
Turn him around, and find a _____.

Write

Write a description of this backward beast. It can be in poem form (such as the descriptions above), or you may write it as a prose description.

The Elidacorc

1. Replace each wrong word.

After three incidence of robbery, the store owner said, "Aisle higher a detective. Maybe the culprit will be cot rite away."

2. Edit the sentence.

dr Watson the assistant to sherlock holmes narrates the story in the Doyles well-known mystery The hound of the baskervilles

I'll shine a little light on this.

3. Choose the correct word.

One of the witnesses to the robbery told (her, their) story on TV.

4. What mood would be set in a story by these phrases?

strange visitors   hushed whispers

a locked corridor   unexplained moans

5. A detective has written a book about his business experiences. From this table of contents, what conclusions can you draw about his business?

Table of Contents

TUESDAY WEEK 7 _____ LANGUAGE PRACTICE

Name

1. Explain the meaning of the sentence.

Hold your tongue about what you heard in the hallway last night.

2. Correct these misspelled words.

negligance   robbary   mistery

investagate   counterfiet   deciet

3. Circle the independent clause.

After she discovered the disappearance of the jewels, she called the police.

4. Finish the poem.

A midnight hour with cold, wet air

And fog that's thick and grey.

Shadows lurk beneath the stair

_____

5. Number these in alphabetical order.

☐ THE CASE OF THE INVISIBLE TEACHER

☐ The Quick Case of the Missing Teeth

☐ THE CASE OF THE CLEVER CATERER

☐ The Case of Twelve Cracked Mirrors

☐ The Curious Case of the Bubbling Bank

☐ THE CASE CRACKED BY THE PARROT

Look for the clues.

Use It! Don't Lose It! IP 612-2

1. It is likely that **duplicity** might be a characteristic of a suspect in a forgery?

2. Place parentheses correctly.

Except for the case on Tuesday morning the investigation of the missing tacos the detective had a quiet week.

3. Circle the appositive in each sentence.

   a. Miss Marple, a clever detective, solved cases by eavesdropping on conversations.

   b. No one knows the whereabouts of the crook Slippery Sal.

   c. We found an important clue, fingerprints on the windowsill.

4. What technique does the writer use in the last sentence of question five?

911? I want to report a break-in.

5. Make an inference about what happened before the events in the passage.

I could only wander in a daze and stare in disbelief. Every drawer was open. Every cupboard was emptied. Dishes, clothes, food, and supplies of every kind were strewn around the house. Overturned couches, chairs, mattresses, and pillows had been slashed. Wastebaskets were dumped; even the bathroom cupboard had been emptied. Boxes, books, bottles, and broken glass surrounded me. Fumbling, stumbling, bumbling—I numbly dialed 911.

1. Finish the analogy.

_____ : investigation :: mystery : mysterious

2. Correct the misspelled words.

Acordding to the restrant owner, fourty freshly baked pies were stollen.

3. Write the sentence in past tense.

"My business is ruined!" cries the baker.

4. Rewrite the passage to give it more sensory appeal.

When Detective Samantha Sleuth came upon the scene of the robbery, the first thing she noticed was the strange smell.

5. How could someone reach Sam Snoop on Friday at 7:00 A.M.?

Sam is a good egg . . . but he's hardboiled.

Sam Snoop's Private Investigations, Inc.

We'll look into

. . . missing persons

. . . stolen properties

. . . troublesome phone calls

. . . and other odd circumstances

licensed, confidential services

Office Open

Tues - Sat, 9 AM - 8 PM

Emergency Phone #333-3333

Name

Read

Read the story once for enjoyment. Read it a second time to identify each of the elements of the story shown on the table below.

The Case of the Serial Bather

It was after the third incident that Detective Razor was asked to take on the cases. Right away, he could see that something strange was happening in Oak Grove. Citizens had called the police to report that they had come home to find dirty bathtubs, with greasy rings left around them. While Detective Razor was amused, he was also concerned enough to investigate the cases thoroughly.

He took the statements of all the homeowners. In each case, the report was that, after being gone on vacation, they came home to find a tub full of dirty water, a bathtub ring, a wet and dirty bath mat, and many long blond hairs around the tub and bathroom. Over the next three weeks, calls kept coming into the police station. The reports were always the same. The scene was always the same. The evidence was always the same.

For a while, the detective was stumped. What a strange "crime"! Why would someone want to take a bath in other peoples' homes? Was it someone who had no bathtub? How did the bather know that the people were away? Why was there no sign of breaking and entering at any of the houses? Razor could only see two links among the cases: the incidents occurred while the homeowners were away, and each home had a pet that was left at home. He had a hunch, so he decided to try something unusual.

Without much trouble, he convinced his neighbor, Janey Green, to take a vacation. Janey made all her arrangements and left town. The detective carefully slipped into her home and settled into the bathroom closet with his lunch and a pillow. He waited. Early the next morning, he heard a key in the back door. Janey's puppy barked excitedly. Razor heard barking and scampering of feet. Soon the bathroom door opened. "Okay, Lucy, time for your bath," came a young man's voice. A teenage boy filled the tub with warm water, added some liquid soap, and helped an old, long-haired blonde dog into the tub. "You soak while I feed and walk Poppy. When I come back, you'll be nice and clean." The big dog was left to bathe while the dog-walker did his job with the vacationer's pet. The case was solved!

Write

Write a short description or explanation for each story element.

I'm on the case.

Theme	
Tone	
Point of View	
Setting	
Main Character	
Plot (include conflict and resolution)	

Name

1. Add correct punctuation.

Ecuador a country whose name means "equator" is located on the equator.

2. Give the meanings of the bold words.

From the top of a mountain in Honduras, I can **spot** my favorite **spot** on the coast.

3. Circle the predicate noun.

Botswana is home to the Kalahari Desert.

4. Identify the mode of writing in question five.

    a. imaginative   c. expository

    b. narrative   d. persuasive

5. What is the letter's main idea?

March 3, 2005

Dear Jannelle,

You are missing an amazing experience by not joining me in this breath-taking country. Here in Nepal, the Himalayas rise sharply to thousands of feet above the valley. Lush forests flow part way up the mountains. Then the sharp white peaks, covered with snow and glaciers, loom like silent giants—ever present, ever splendid. This is like no other place I have ever been. You would love it here; you could take magnificent pictures. You must come with me next time!

Start planning,

Maxie

Name

1. Write the plural of each word.

volcano   key   library   halo

2. If you want to find information on the political history of the European nation of Georgia, what reference source would be useful?

3. Choose a pair of antonyms.

  ○ schism – split   ○ intrepid – cowardly

  ○ menace – threaten ○ dispel – scatter

4. Which phrase means **the beauty of several islands**?

    a. the island's beauties

    b. the islands' beauties

    c. the island's beauty

    d. the islands' beauty

Smile!

5. Add a title to this passage.

_____

A first visit to Fiji is unlikely to be the last. Usually, first-timers are delightfully surprised to find the perfect combination of quiet sunny relaxation, exotic sounds and sights, and exhilarating outdoor water activities. Long, white beaches, warm night breezes, slow palm tree afternoons, many hours a year of sunshine, unique dining experiences, and adventure on the South Pacific capture their spirits. Most visitors leave Fiji's islands longing to return.

1. Cross out unnecessary words.

There are no nations that don't have no neighbors other than Russia or China.

2. The sentence below is an example of

   a. idiom   c. simile

   b. hyperbole   d. personification

With dozens of lucrative gold mines in her back pocket, South Africa is as rich as a queen.

3. Correct the misspelled words.

parallel	innacent	ocurr
nesessary	canoe	laundary

4. What is the connotation of the word **island**?

I wonder if I packed my water wings?

5. Do you think that the tourists will be able to see all the islands in one week?

The Island Quest

When we learned that the country of Vanuatu is an archipelago of 83 islands, we wanted to see them all in the seven days we had to spend in the country. We hired a boat and set forth, maps in hand. On the first day, we sailed by 15 islands. We saw 18 more on the second day. The third day, the winds were so still that we used the motor, getting to only seven islands. Our plan was to see the remaining islands in the next three days, leaving a whole day to hurry back to our starting point. The fourth day, a furious storm was brewing. Our sailboat was too small to brave the waves.

THURSDAY WEEK 8 _____ LANGUAGE PRACTICE
Name

1. Correctly capitalize and punctate this story title:
stranded in the costa rican rainforest

2. Cross out words that are not compounds.

wonderful   submersible   friendless

footloose   Mapquest   noteworthy

3. Circle the object pronouns.

Will you and he be flying to Portugal with her and me?

4. What part of speech is the word **atoll**?

5. Write two similarities and two differences between the two countries.

I can't decide where to go.

Guatemala
Area: 108,890 sq. mi.
Population: 14,281,000
Location: Central America
Water Borders: Pacific Ocean, Caribbean Sea
Neighbors: Mexico, Honduras, Belize, El Salvador

Belize
Area: 22,960 sq. mi.
Population: 273,000
Location: Central America
Water Borders: Caribbean Sea
Neighbors: Mexico, Guatemala

Read

1. What two names are used for the world's smallest nation?
2. About how many people live in Iceland?
3. What nations share the island of Hispaniola?
4. Which country is home to many gorillas?
5. Which fact is the one you'd like most to research further? Why?

Some Interesting Facts About Some World Nations

The currency in Malaysia is the ringgit.

The Sahara Desert covers 85 percent of Algeria.

East Timor is one of the world's newest countries (2002).

South Korea is home to one of the fastest-growing cities in the world (Ansan).

Indonesia has the largest number of active volcanoes.

Canada has the longest coastline of any country (202,080 km).

Uganda has the youngest population (50 percent under 15 years old).

The sea has reclaimed 40 percent of the land in the Netherlands.

Vatican City, also called Holy See, is the world's smallest nation.

A national park in Rwanda is home to half of the remaining gorillas in the world.

There are more than 100 volcanoes in Iceland, one for every 2,822 people.

For many years, Barbary pirates used Algiers as their home base.

Haiti shares the island Hispaniola with another country (Dominican Republic).

The ruler of Brunei is one of the world's richest people. His name is Sultan Sir Muda Hassanal Bolkiah Mu'izzadin Waddaulah.

Write

Use some of the ideas collected in the web to write a descriptive paragraph about Barbados. Include a clear topic sentence, details, a good beginning, and a conclusion.

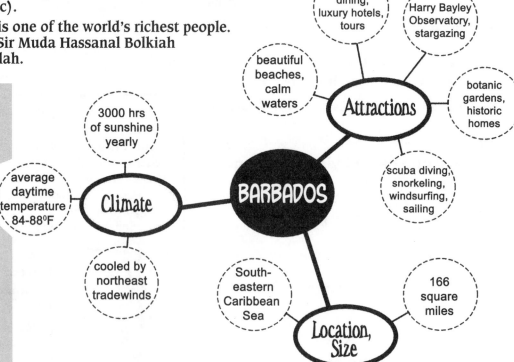

- BARBADOS
- Climate
  - 3000 hrs of sunshine yearly
  - average daytime temperature 84-88°F
  - cooled by northeast tradewinds
- Attractions
  - shopping, dining, luxury hotels, tours
  - Harry Bayley Observatory, stargazing
  - beautiful beaches, calm waters
  - botanic gardens, historic homes
  - scuba diving, snorkeling, windsurfing, sailing
- Location, Size
  - South-eastern Caribbean Sea
  - 166 square miles

1. Choose the correct word.

The matador waved his cape with smooth, **(graceful, gracious)** movements.

2. Edit the sentence.

bullfighting is a popular sport in portugal southern france and many Spanish-speaking countries such as spain and mexico

3. Underline any adjectives and draw a box around any adverbs.

See how he skillfully maneuvers the charging bull by moving the red cape?

4. Which example shows personification?

   a. The red cape invites the bull to come closer.

   b. Dust billowed and hooves pounded as the bull pushed against the gates.

5. Follow directions to finish the picture.

Draw a cape in the matador's hands.
Add detail and decoration to his clothes.
Draw a tail on the bull.
Draw hot breath coming out of the bull's nostrils.

1. What is the meaning of the underlined word?

Usually the bullfight lasts much longer, but this one was <u>truncated</u> by the injury of the matador in the opening minutes.

2. Write the sentence in past tense.

The matador runs, leaps, and falls as the bull tries to gore him.

Ole!

3. Circle the participle.

Did the angry bull, charging with its tremendous weight, really terrify the matador?

4. Which of these words would be found between dictionary guidewords: **bullfight** and **bungle**?

   ○ bull   ○ bully   ○ bullet

   ○ bunk   ○ bed   ○ bumble

5. Write a brief summary of this passage.

In early July, people from all over the world head for Pamplona, Spain, to run with the bulls. The race takes place each morning from July 17 – July 14. At precisely 8:00 a.m., a rocket is launched to signal the opening of the corral gates. Six wild bulls and two herds of tame bulls run through the streets of the town toward the bull ring. The run only lasts a few minutes, but the crowds and the speed of the bulls make it a dangerous sport. Even with the strict rules, over 200 runners have been injured, and several people have been killed.

1. What punctuation belongs after the greeting in a friendly letter?

2. Which would a matador try to do to a bull?

   ○ divulge   ○ vanquish   ○ acquit   ○ condole

3. Circle the letters of correct examples.

   a. Whoever fights bulls is brave.

   b. Juan and him want to be matadors.

   c. Come to the bull ring with Maria and I.

   d. Doesn't she want to join you and me?

4. Which is likely to include descriptive writing?

   ○ brochure inviting runners to Pamplona, Spain

   ○ list of rules for the bull run

   ○ recipe for Spanish flan (custard)

   ○ job application for a matador job

5. What do you think is the reason behind rules 3 and 4?

Bull-Run Rules

1 Runners must be 18 or older.
2 Runners must stay within official zones.
3 Doors of all houses along the bull run must be closed.
4 Observers must not hide in doorways or corners along the course.
5 Persons under the influence of alcohol or drugs are disqualified.
6 Runners must wear clothes and shoes that will not impede safe running.
7 Do not call or distract the bulls.
8 Do not stop in the bull run.
9 Do not grab or harass the bulls.

I'm getting out of here!

1. Circle the prefix meaning *outside of*.

   expel   antonym   regress   Internet

2. Is this book likely to be fiction, nonfiction, or biography?

Maybe I could fight a beetle?

How To Fight Bulls Safely
Matt T. Doer

3. Correct each sentence.

   a. This here bull is the fiercest.

   b. Where is the matador at?

   c. Carlos Arruza, he is one of the world's greatest matadors.

   d. You shouldn't of run with the bulls.

4. Add **-ed** and **-ing** to each word to make two new words. Spell the new words correctly.

   simplify   argue   hum

5. Edit the passage.

   bullfighting is a Contest between a bull and a Matador, the fight begins with a trumpit fanfare and the releese of the Bull. the matador's helper's called banderilleros wave a cape to get the bull to charge. using the cape the matador guides the bull past his body a few times. Then picadors on horseback force lances into the bull's neck Banderilleros enter again: to place wooden sticks with sharp steel points behind the bull's neck. By the time the matador enters the ring agin the bull is weakened and the matador kills it with a sword: the whole fight takes about 20 minutes?

Name

Read

1. How many different matadors are mentioned in the poems?
2. What is the theme of the selections?
3. What is the author's purpose for writing these poems?
4. What is your favorite limerick? Tell why.
5. One limerick is out of order. Number the lines in the correct order.

Deseo ser un matador.

A bull has the name of Raoul,
And the people of Spain call him, "Cool!"
His stomping was fearful,
His snort was an earful,
Anyone who fights him's a fool.

"I can outsmart that old bull, no doubt!"
Said Sue with an arrogant shout.
The fight wasn't her first,
But it sure was her worst.
On a stretcher they carried her out.

I waved my cape like a brave matador
As I did, I could hear the crowd roar.
Then the bull spied the red
And he lowered his head.
Without thinking, I ran for the door.

Tried to outwit a bull yesterday.
A shy matador named Jose
His shoulder was torn
But the crowd just kept shouting, "Ole!"
By the creature's right horn,

A man bought a bull in Madrid
As a pet for Alberto, his kid.
In spite of their adoring,
The bull started goring,
So they traded it in for a squid.

Write

Take the point of view of a reporter attending a bullfight. Write a description of the matador's (or the bull's) behavior.

1. What is the meaning of the underlined word?

I've read so many tall tales in the last year that I'm ready to take a <u>hiatus</u> for a few months and read something different.

2. Write the words correctly.

definately   allmost

buzy   exxagerate

3. Circle the nouns. Underline the verbs.

Last summer, the temperatures soared so high that corn popped right on the cobs.

4. Name the audience for the preview.

Cluck!

Welcome to your new home, the city of Southfield. Here's a preview of our weather. In the summer, it gets so hot that the farmers feed ice to their hens to keep them from laying hard-boiled eggs.

5. What effective techniques does the author use in telling this story?

Let me tell you about last year's big storm. The wind was so strong that it blew the feathers right off the chickens and the worms out of their holes. Birds had to fly backwards to keep dirt out of their eyes. The force of the wind moved the county and kept the sun from moving across the sky. The sunset was delayed by five hours. One woman made the mistake of opening her mouth, and the wind blew her whole body up like a balloon.

1. Edit the sentence.

Pecos bill the gratest cowboy of all time fell out of his familys wagun and wuz left behind read the teacher to her students

2. Correct the error.

The tales about Pecos Bill shows his amazing strength and courage.

3. Which word completes the analogy?

warm : scorching :: _____ : frigid

     a. frozen   b. bitter

     c. cool   d. sultry

4. Choose the correct words.

They say Pecos Bill handled rattlesnakes (real, really) (good, well).

I've told a tall tale or two.

5. What kind of book is this?

Index
beanstalk, 500-ft, 113
Bunyan, Paul, 44–46
Crocket, Davy, 50–52
extreme temperatures, 19–24
frogs, raining, 62
it was so cold that, 19–20
it was so hot that, 22–24
lumberjacks, giant, 44–48
mosquitoes, giant, 72
Pecos Bill, 55–58
shadows, frozen, 25
spiders, man-sized, 77
storms, outrageous, 58–60
whoppers, 1–12

1. Circle the simple subject. Underline the complete predicate.

The Santa Fe spider has 100 legs, a gigantic forked tail, and fangs bigger than a rattlesnake's.

2. Write two antonyms for **fallacy**.

3. Add the endings. Spell each new word correctly.

love + ly = _____

rude + er = _____

plot + ed = _____

drip + ing = _____

4. The sentence contains an example of
○ hyperbole   ○ alliteration   ○ rhyme
○ metaphor   ○ onomatopoeia   ○ simile

Slippery snakes circling, hissing, sneering, swallowed each other's tails.

5. Name two features that the two characters have in common.

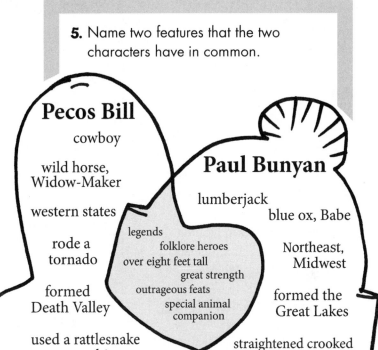

Pecos Bill
cowboy
wild horse, Widow-Maker
western states
rode a tornado
formed Death Valley
used a rattlesnake as a whip

Paul Bunyan
lumberjack
blue ox, Babe
Northeast, Midwest
formed the Great Lakes
straightened crooked rivers

legends
folklore heroes
over eight feet tall
great strength
outrageous feats
special animal companion

1. Write and define a homonym for each word.
rain   board   principle   patience

2. Add apostrophes where they belong.

a mans fish stories

a scissors handles

three tall tales titles

one familys whoppers

3. Rewrite the sentence to clarify the meaning.
Susannah took a picture of a ten-foot-tall mosquito using her new digital camera.

4. Put these words in alphabetical order.

lies	literal	libel
lessons	lying	loosely

That's what I call breaking the ice.

5. Write a good headline for the story.

_____

_____

A local family has just revealed a surprising story about last winter's severe temperatures. In January, Mrs. Maggie Smith called her son to come home for dinner. But her son did not hear her until late March. According to scientists, it was so cold that her words froze before they could reach the boy. Three months later, when the words thawed, the boy heard his mother calling. So, he went home for dinner.

Name

Read

1. What details are given to describe Paul's ox?

2. How much food does Paul need in a six-day work week?

3. What natural wonder did Paul claim to create?

4. What information on the application is most surprising to you?

My mother was a tree.

Write

Write a news article about an incident that might have involved this huge, strong character. Include a strong headline, an inviting beginning, and a satisfying conclusion

JOB APPLICATION – Position: Lumberjack	
Name	*Paul Bunyan*
Age	*24*
Height	*8 ft, 11 in*
Weight	*410 lbs*
Physical Condition	*superb*
Birth Date, Place	*July 1, 1880; Maine*
Past Work Experience	*wood splitting, tree-felling, tree-climbing, and lumberjack work across America; created the Great Lakes with my footprints*
Abilities, Qualities Related to the Job	*- tremendous strength and endurance* *- 6 years experience in all kinds of terrain* *- can fell two trees with one swing of axe* *- can chop trees 16 hours without stopping* *- companion ox, Babe, has horn span of 42 axe handles*
Preferred Working Conditions	*prefer to work with my blue ox; he increases amount of work that can be done in a day—can haul great quantities of wood at one time*
Special Needs or Requirements	*need boots size 40; need supply of food equaling 18,000 calories a day; need 30 lb of grain a day for my ox*
References	*American Timber Company; Continental Timber Company; U.S. President*

1. Which sentence shows correct usage?

   a. Whoever owns that parrot is lucky.

   b. The iguana owner is the one whom bought the parrot and the cockatiel.

2. Place dashes where they belong in this sentence.

Seventy-five percent of pet owners you may not believe this sign their pet's name to their greeting cards.

3. Finish each word to make it a compound.

cat _____   _____ worm

_____ bird   dog _____

4. How many of the pets listed are in the cat family?

5. What is the setting in this passage?

What a lazy snake you are! You lie around, snoozing, basking in the warm light and secure home of your terrarium. The only effort you put forth is slithering slowly around, pressing your skin against the warm glass. And, oh, yes, you do also open your jaw now and then. That's when the top slides back and a fat mouse is dropped into your cozy glass home just in time for your dinner.

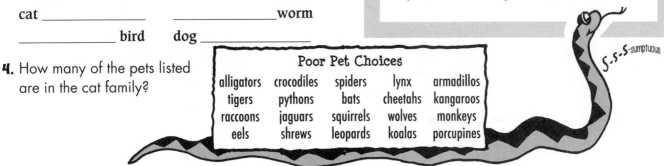

S-s-s-sumptuous

Poor Pet Choices

alligators	crocodiles	spiders	lynx	armadillos
tigers	pythons	bats	cheetahs	kangaroos
raccoons	jaguars	squirrels	wolves	monkeys
eels	shrews	leopards	koalas	porcupines

1. Where might a dog owner find a **polynomial**?

   ○ in a pet store   ○ on a caboose

   ○ in a stew   ○ under a mattress

   ○ in a math book   ○ at church

2. Circle the correct word.

Every time Georgia tries to catch her frog, the pet (eludes, alludes) her.

3. Which contains an **infinitive phrase**?

   a. Alex really wanted to own a pet skunk.

   b. Getting a ferret was Abby's dream.

4. Write three phrases that describe a dog you have seen. Each phrase should appeal strongly to the sense of hearing.

I am doggedly writing an essay about dogs.

5. Read the encyclopedia entry to find what percentage of an iguana's length is taken up by its body (excluding tail).

An iguana is a large lizard found in tropical Central and South America and in the Galapagos Islands. The common iguana lives in trees along streams. This bright green lizard has a crest of spines that run down its back from the neck to its striped tail. The tail is extraordinarily long, taking up two-thirds of the lizard's total length.

1. Explain the meaning of the sentence.

If you want a macaw for a pet, you can expect to pay through the nose.

2. Identify the verb form in the sentence.

    a. infinitive   b. gerund   c. participle

The old caged parrot was a chatty bird named Lillian.

3. Correct the misspelled words.

elegent   fluent   vacant

pheasent   elephunt   apparant

4. Which examples contain **similes**?

    a. She chatters like a cage full of monkeys.

    b. Her room is as cluttered as the bottom of a birdcage.

    c. My kitty is a gorgeous, preening queen.

5. What is the main idea of this passage?

Who could imagine that dogs would skydive? Brutus, a miniature dachshund, is an impressive diver. He has taken well over 70 jumps accompanied by his owner. This daring dog holds the record for the highest canine sky dive with a jump from 15,000 feet!

Call me Super Dog.

1. Edit the sentence.

prudel the parrot knew 800 English words her favorite sentence was what are you doing

2. Circle the indirect object.

Don't buy your kids an alligator for a pet.

3. Which word does not belong?

○ animated   ○ lethargic

○ idle   ○ languid

4. Shawn wants a book about a dog breeder named Horatio Hound. Which kinds of searches should he do in the library catalog?

    a. subject   b. title   c. author

Sometimes I parrot my own words.

5. Identify the bias in the selection. Then write a conclusion for the essay.

This is some of the most outlandish, unbelievable pet information yet. Some cat owners actually arranged an expensive wedding for their pets. Spending an outlandish $16,000, one cat owner, Wichan Jaratarcha, hosted a feline wedding at an expensive discotheque in Thailand. The story gets even more ludicrous: The two rare "diamond-eye" cats, Phet and Ploy, wore matching pink outfits.

Read

1. What is the purpose of these selections?
2. What is the intended audience?
3. Name a feature mentioned about ferrets but not about rats.
4. Name three similarities between the pets.
5. What might be the biggest drawback to each as a pet?

Ferrets As Pets

- can fit into a small multi-level cage
- need lots of time to run around
- name means "little thief"; they find and hide small things
- some counties ban ownership of ferrets
- do not get along with hamsters, guinea pigs, rabbits
- can be trained to use a litter box
- cute—adorable, unusual faces, big eyes
- smart and playful; will play with other ferrets or with humans
- each has distinct personality
- quiet, little vocalization
- cuddly, affectionate
- food is easy to obtain

Rats As Pets

- big enough to be sturdy and small enough for a child to hold
- social animals; love to be held and cuddled
- smart—learn quickly, love to show off
- can learn to climb a ladder or run a maze
- cute with shiny fur, cute ears, and dark eyes
- can fit into a small cage
- easy to care for
- need little space
- food is easy to find
- come in a variety of colors and patterns
- nocturnal; love to run around at night
- short life span $2\frac{1}{2}$ to 3 years

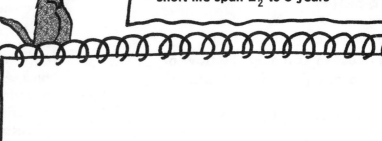

Write

Write an argument that will convince a reader to consider either a ferret or a rat for a pet, *or* argue against having the animals as pets.

1. Which sentence is correct?

    a. Did you and him see that lightning?

    b. Static electricity made her and mine hair stand on end.

    c. We and they built electrical circuits.

    d. She and me are electricians.

2. Choose words with a suffix meaning **the act or process of**.

    ○ electrify   ○ failure   ○ vacation   ○ explosion

3. Which selection is probably imaginative?

    ○ tale of a cowboy who rides lightning bolts

    ○ advertisement for a tiny flashlight

    ○ explanation of how a circuit works

4. Circle the silent letters.

    gnat   **knickers**

    scheme   **gourmet**

Shocking!

5. a. Does the selection provide enough material to draw a conclusion about why the parade was discontinued?

    b. Estimate the total number of people who watched the parade.

A magnificent electrical parade was a regular feature at Disneyland between 1972 and 1996. This fantastic event displayed floats covered by thousands of lights coordinated to a symphonic sound track. The Main Street Electrical Parade was performed 3,600 times—each time before approximately 20,000 viewers. It had 26 features with 575,000 lights in seven different colors.

1. Explain what needs to be done to capitalize and punctuate this book title correctly.

    disneys main street electrical parade a history

2. Underline the prepositional phrase(s).

    A circuit breaker can stop the flow of electricity to any part of the house.

3. What is the denotation of **lightning**?

4. Which is the best key word or phrase for an encyclopedia search on the topic of electronically-produced music?

    ○ electronics   ○ electricity   ○ music

    ○ guitars   ○ electronic music ○ keyboards

5. Edit the passage.

    most people have experiensed an electrac charge it happins when you walk accross a carpet and touch a metal doorknob.

    Or when you take off a wool cap and your hair stands on end all matter has adoms: All adoms contain electracaly charged particals protons and electrons. When they are rubbed electrons jump from one objekt to another cauzing a charge.

My music is electrifying!

1. Write the plural form.

tattoo	ferry	tablespoon
glass	mouse	father-in-law
canopy	cello	superhero

2. Could a scientist give an **oration** on electricity?

3. Add correct punctuation.

One power plant provided electricity for 160000 homes another produced electricity for fewer than 100000 homes.

4. What stereotype is reflected?

Some people choose to "get off the grid" (to refrain from using electricity provided by utility companies). Obviously, such people are anti-social, or hostile to the government and business.

You light up my life.

Thanks, I try my best.

5. For each statement, write **O** (opinion) or **F** (fact).

_____ Electricity can be made from solar power.

_____ Burning coal is not the best way to produce electricity.

_____ Burning coal is a common way to produce electricity.

_____ An electrician's job is easy.

_____ Thomas Edison owned the first power plant.

_____ Benjamin Franklin proved that lightning contained electrical power.

_____ Every nation should use more wind and solar power.

1. Write the sentence in past tense.

The Disneyland Main Street Electrical Parade uses over 27 tons of batteries, lights, and other equipment.

2. Seeing the electric parade was the highlight of our 1995 visit to Disneyland. Was this the **nadir** or **zenith** of our visit?

3. Add **ance** or **ence** to complete each word.

neglig _____ occur _____ abund _____

evid _____ accept _____ abs _____

4. Which reference will provide several synonyms for the word **amazement**?

The Wizard of Menlo Park

Enlightening!

5. Add a topic sentence.

_____

_____

Although this was the first central power plant ever built, it did not have a difficult beginning. The Pearl Street Station grew fast and inspired an entire industry. The owner, Thomas Edison, opened the plant in 1882 with one generator that produced enough electricity to light 800 light bulbs. Within a year, energy for 12,000 bulbs was produced. Today, power plants can keep five billion lights going.

Read

Follow the clues to complete the puzzle. Except for 11 down, the words all name things that use electricity.

Across

3. rail transportation
4. they magnify your music
5. cools in hot weather
7. seagoing vessels
8. crisps your bread
9. talk while you walk
12. mini pool, warm water
13. screened entertainment
14. helps figure your math
16. dentist's tool

Down

1. scooter for the ocean
2. magnifies tiny things
5. portable illumination
6. presses clothing
8. moving walk at the gym
10. takes you up ten floors
11. to infuse with electricity
15. micro-___ (for computers)

Snap! Crackle! POP!

Working crosswords makes me cross-eyed.

Write

Finish each "electric" joke by completing the question or the answer. Use your creativity to make the jokes clever. Be sure they have some relationship to the topic of electricity.

What did the electrician say when he met his friends?

Watts up?

WHAT DID...

THAT MUST HAVE BEEN AN ELECTRIFYING EXPERIENCE.

Why does the battery repairman carry lots of credit cards?

She puts on her shoes and shocks.

1. Write an antonym for each word on the list in this sign.

We Cannot Admit Anyone Who Is...

scrawny   parsimonious
boisterous   punctual
adroit   sensitive

That's funny!

2. Edit the sentence.

my friend moe does exactly the opposite of everything I do said joe

3. The _____ of a written selection is the approach a writer takes toward the topic.

○ theme   ○ plot   ○ tone   ○ mood   ○ conflict

4. Choose the sentence type.

○ imperative   ○ interrogative   ○ exclamatory

What a coincidence that was!

5. What will happen next?

Luke was tired of being the shortest clown in the circus. He was always paired up with Leon, the tallest clown, and the crowd laughed at him and teased him. He decided to be tall instead of small. In preparation for the next show, Luke taped a tall can on top of a two-foot-high box. He used string and tape to attach some wooden stilts on top of the can. He found a ladder and got ready to get up on those stilts and be taller than Leon.

1. Spell each word correctly.

evning   brillyant   modarete
moorning   shadowey   extreem

2. Circle any linking verbs. Underline any predicate adjectives.

Copper is pliable, but glass is brittle.

3. Why would these be in the same class?

contrary   opposed   antagonistic
differing   adverse   converse

4. Cross out unnecessary words.

Niagara Falls it may seem like the most tallest waterfall until you compare it with another waterfall called Angel Falls.

5. Compare the short tower to the tall tower. Describe three differences.

Eiffel Tower
1052 ft

Which one should I climb first?

The Leaning Tower of Pisa
108 ft

1. Which examples are correct?

    a. All snails moves slowly.

    b. Cheetahs run faster than other animals.

    c. Ducks flies 13 times faster than woodcocks.

    d. Dolphins can't swim as fast as sailfish.

2. What is the theme of the limerick in question five?

3. Choose pairs that are synonyms.

    ○ altercation – quarrel   ○ vigilant – watchful

    ○ discrete – careless   ○ convene – gather

4. Circle the correctly spelled words.

hopeing	useable	lovely
skating	hopless	truly
rubing	stopped	floped

5. Number the lines in to put them in correct sequence.

  ___ Is not the opposite of near,

  ___ You'd be wrong; you wouldn't be right.

  ___ Day is the opposite of night.

  ___ If you think far from here

  ___ And dark is the opposite of light.

I meant to draw a straight line – but I did just the opposite.

1. Put these in alphabetical order.

fast	narrow	straight	lost
slow	wide	crooked	found

2. Correct the sentences.

Scarcely no animal is as tall as a giraffe, but don't worry none about feeling sorry for that short beetle. He has a powerful sting.

3. Would you put a **cliché** on a salad?

4. Correct any misspelled words.

Antartica looks quiet oppisite from Afraca. One is icey; the other is coverd with sand and thik forrests.

5. Revise the sentences for clarity.

    a. When Mike and Tyson jumped from the hot tub into a snowbank, he shouted, "Yikes!"

    b. While dreaming about skydiving and scuba diving, the telephone started ringing.

    c. Mice ran across our tent floor while telling stories about the best and worst moments of the day.

Go left!

NO, go right!

Read

1. What do you notice about the first and last lines of the poem?

2. What words describe movements?

3. How does the author contrast the pace of day and night?

4. What word means **the period between day and night**?

DAY
Bright, warm
Waking, moving, bustling
Dawn, sunshine, shadows, dusk
Yawning, slowing, quieting
Dark, still
NIGHT

Write

Create your own diamond poem of opposites (diamante).

1. The first and last lines name the opposites: hot and cold.

2. On line 2, write two adjectives to describe hot.

3. On line 3, write three participles (verbs ending in -ing) about hot.

4. On line 4, write four nouns—two associated with hot, then two associated with cold.

5. On line 5, write three participles about cold.

6. On line 6, write two adjectives to describe cold.

HOT

_____

_____

_____

_____

_____

COLD

Use It! Don't Lose It! IP 612-2

1. Choose the literary technique used in the example.

○ alliteration   ○ hyperbole   ○ imagery

The princess prefers that plenty of perfume be prepared for her pyramid.

2. Write the singular form of each noun.

○ pillows   ○ mummies   ○ tens

○ wives   ○ valuables   ○ dignitaries

3. Which examples show correct usage?

a. Where in the tomb does the mummy lay?

b. She has laid here for 4,000 years.

c. I saw a mummy lying in the museum!

4. What is the main idea?

Don't leave Egypt without visiting the Great Sphinx. It is a statue of astounding size with a human head and a lion's body. You'll be amazed by this 4,500-year-old stone carving.

5. Read each comment made inside a pyramid. Write a homonym for one of the words in each.

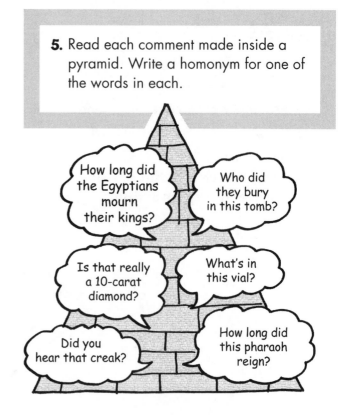

How long did the Egyptians mourn their kings?

Who did they bury in this tomb?

Is that really a 10-carat diamond?

What's in this vial?

Did you hear that creak?

How long did this pharaoh reign?

1. Put correct punctuation in the box.

The ancient Egyptians were the first people known to have made something that is a regular part of today's cuisine ☐ leavened bread.

2. What is the meaning of the roots of the words **mortify** and **immortal**?

3. Count the common and proper nouns.

The Nile River was the lifeblood of ancient Egypt. Fertile soil along the river provided a rich setting for a good food supply.

4. Would *pharoah* be found on a dictionary page with the guide words **phylum** and **picturesque**?

The Egyptians invented paper.

Aren't you glad?

5. Summarize this passage.

Ancient Egyptians believed that they could enjoy life after death. Because of this belief, they preserved dead bodies so they would not decay. In addition, before death, Egyptians built tombs and filled them with items they imagined they might need in the afterlife. They stored clothing, food, jewelry, and other valuables. Wealthy Egyptians even kept statues of servants in their tombs so they would have someone to wait on them after death.

1. Add the ending to each word. Spell the new word correctly.

fancy + er =   final + ly =

lie + ed =   like + able =

2. The underlined words are a _____ phrase.
- ○ gerund   ○ prepositional
- ○ participial   ○ infinitive

A major achievement of the ancient Egyptians was <u>studying medicine</u> and the human body.

3. A written explanation of how to build a pyramid would be written in which mode?
- ○ descriptive   ○ expository   ○ imaginative
- ○ narrative   ○ persuasive   ○ personal

4. What is the meaning of the underlined word?

Paintings on the walls of tombs <u>depicted</u> scenes from ancient Egyptian society. This helped archaeologists learn about the culture.

5. Follow the directions.
- Get a sheet of drawing paper.
- Draw a two-dimensional view of the inside of a pyramid.
- Divide it into three levels.
- Draw two statues and three tall urns on the first level.
- Draw three mummies on the second level.
- On the third level, draw a table with jewels and other valuable items.

I'm stuck on Step 2.

1. What reference source contains histories of word origins?

2. Add apostrophes where needed.

Whats the most interesting fact youve learned about the Egyptians culture?

3. Finish the analogy.

girlfriend : _____ :: lifetime : timeless

4. Circle the independent clause.

By observing natural cycles in geography and astrology, the Egyptians were able to develop a calendar.

I'm well-preserved.

5. Write a topic sentence.

_____

_____

These structures are their most famous achievement. They stand as striking reminders of the glory of ancient Egyptian culture. The dry climate has preserved the pyramids for over 4,000 years. Because of this, the 400-foot-tall tombs still stand, reminding the modern world of the amazing skills and sophistication of this ancient society.

Name

HOW TO MAKE A MUMMY

Read

1. What step comes just before the body is wrapped in strips of linen?

2. What is the chemical used for embalming a mummy?

3. What part of the process probably takes the most work?

4. Why do you think the brain was not kept?

5. What step comes before the packing of the body with an embalming chemical?

1. Remove the brain through the nose and throw it away.

2. Remove all the internal organs.

The organs are saved in Coptic jars.

3. Pack the inside of the body with an embalming substance called natron.

4. Pack the body entirely with a layer of natron and let it dry for 40 days.

5. After 40 days, wrap the body in strips of linen moistened with resin glue.

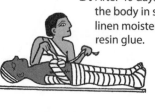

6. Wrap the body in 20 or more layers.

7. Place into three coffins.

I love my mummy.

Write

Choose three topics. Write an inviting beginning sentence or two for a story on each topic.

- a mummy that showed up at school
- a whole pyramid that went missing
- three friends who went to Egypt to talk to the Great Sphinx
- a tour of the pyramids that did not go according to plan
- the talking camel that rescued lost desert travelers
- a young woman of ancient Egypt who had no intention of becoming queen

1. Edit the sentence.

what could explain the disappearance of awhole village joe labelle wondered when he discovered that all 2000 people were gone

2. In the sentence above, what caused Joe Labelle to be puzzled?

3. Write a possessive phrase that means

a. the disappearance of a village

b. the questions of searchers

c. the journey of five searchers

d. the questions of one searcher

I've never even been to Bermuda.

4. Circle the correct word.

Some people think green flashes, sparks of green seen above the horizon at sunset, are an optical (**illusion, allusion, delusion**).

5. Which examples contain a pun?

a. The ship was snatched by cloud fingers.

b. Do visitors from outer space go to school at a "universe"-ity?

c. Sailors always wave as their ships sail away.

d. Did you say your backyard is like the Bermuda Triangle?

e. There are UFOs in the parking lot? Now, that's an alien idea!

1. Circle the prepositional phrase.

Many planes, ships, and small boats reportedly have disappeared into the Bermuda Triangle

I avoid the Triangle.

2. Correct the misspelled words.

tropicle   channel   vessel

futile   hystericle   candal

3. What is the connotation of **disappearance**?

4. Which reference source is a book of maps?

a. an almanac

b. a geographical dictionary

c. an atlas

d. an encyclopedia

5. Write three questions you would like to ask the navy officials who investigated this disappearance.

The disappearance of Flight 19, a squadron of five U.S. Navy bombers, is one of the most repeated Bermuda Triangle stories. The planes were on a training flight from Fort Lauderdale, Florida, on December 15, 1945, when they flew into the clouds and were never seen again. According to the author of a best-selling book on the Bermuda Triangle, the planes simply disappeared. A navy seaplane sent to the rescue also disappeared. The incidents have never been fully explained.

1. Give the meaning of each prefix.

a. withdraw _____

b. kilometer _____

c. transpolar _____

d. extraterrestrial _____

2. Add capital letters where necessary.

dr. j. allen hynek, an astronomer consultant to the u.s. air force, formed a long, precise definition of a ufo.

3. Write the comparative and superlative forms of the adjective **well**.

comparative = _____

superlative = _____

4. What is the intended audience for a pamphlet that explains how to sail safely across the Bermuda Triangle?

How far did Niagara fall?

5. Read the passage carefully. Then rewrite it in your own words.

The Day The Falls Stopped Falling

It really happened! Niagara Falls actually stopped flowing for several hours on March 29, 1848. Some people say that the falls froze over from the extreme cold winter temperatures. But that is not what happened. An ice jam in the Niagara River above the falls stopped the flow. The riverbed became dry enough that people walked around on it, picking up artifacts dropped by the water.

1. Correct the language usage.

It is well that you saw that UFO when it landed. You reacted good by reporting it.

2. What part of a book is an alphabetical listing of all the topics in the book, accompanied by the page numbers?

3. Circle the correctly spelled words.

yacht   **criuse**

Atlantick   **dissappear**

4. One word is used three times. Give the meaning for each use of that word.

Did you watch the UFO light on the baseball field? Did you see the flashing lights light up the sky?

Hello, 911?

Follow that green flash.

5. Edit the passage.

Some people claim that green flashes are just a Myth. That you can never see one. they are real: but they are rare? A green flash occurrs at sunset when the Sun sudenly changes color from red to blue and; for a few seconds' looks green. a brief ray of green apears to shoot up from the horison, giving the impression of a green flash this only happens in the middle latitudes under specific atmospheric condishuns most people who look for green flashes are not lucky enough to see one.

Read

1. What is the genre (kind of writing) represented by this selection?

2. What is the purpose of the selection?

3. Is there enough evidence to conclude that the Slatter family was the first reported disappearance of the weekend?

4. What was the first disappearance ever reported in the Bermuda Triangle?

Some mysterious events were reported to the Coast Guard in Miami, Florida, last weekend. On Friday morning, the Slatter family of Orlando headed east into the Atlantic Ocean for an afternoon trip on their new 40-foot sailboat. The boat did not return to the marina and has not been found. Several hours later, Sunshine Air Flight 23 from Puerto Rico disappeared on its way to Miami. There has been no sighting of the plane and no radio contact. A third disappearance was reported on Sunday. Relatives watched Patty and Paul McMain parasail into clouds above Bermuda. The couple has not been seen since.

Searchers have covered the area for days. They have found no trace of the boats, the airplane, or the McMains. Ever since the first disappearance of a ship (The U.S.S. Cyclops) in 1918, sailors and scientists have been puzzled by the strange disappearances in this area known as the Bermuda Triangle or the Devil's Triangle.

Mischief in the Triangle

Write

Write a story to match the picture.

1. A series of events that make up a story is the

○ theme ○ plot ○ setting ○ conflict ○ mood

2. Circle the complete subject.

A luxury steamboat, The American Queen, holds 650 people on six passenger decks.

3. Add correct punctuation and capitalization to this closing of a business letter:

yours truly

hoyt d sayle

4. Give a synonym and an antonym for the word **adventuresome**.

5. What is the main idea?

An ordinary ship moves rather slowly through water because a huge part of its hull (bottom) is submerged. This causes a strong drag on the ship as it moves through the water. A hydrofoil, on the other hand, moves quickly. In fact, it is the fastest boat you can find. This boat has a great advantage: It sits above the water, supported by huge wings (foils) that lift it up. A hydrofoil can move at speeds of up to 70 miles per hour as it skims along the surface.

Everything is shipshape with me.

1. Use your dictionary to help you answer the question:

Could you take a synagogue along on a hydrofoil ride?

2. Name the part of speech for each underlined word.

The <u>most</u> important <u>force</u> that <u>drives</u> a sailboat <u>into</u> the wind is <u>suction</u>.

3. What is the meaning of **propulsion**?

a. explosion   c. nausea

b. pushing   d. motion

4. Correct the misspelled words.

memoes   potatoes   defys

sopranoes   legatos   sympathies

I had a submarine sandwich for lunch.

5. Add a title to this passage.

_____

A submarine's name tells what it is: a vessel that can travel under (sub) the water (marine). Its sleek bullet-like shape helps it to slide quickly through the water. A submarine has a pressure hull made of strong steel that can keep the crew and machinery safe. Large tanks can be filled with water to allow the submarine to dive, or emptied to enable resurfacing. Modern nuclear submarines can stay submerged for months, because they are able to provide air for the crew.

1. Edit the passage.

On November 9 2001 Omar Hanapiev pulled a 1269861-pound ship with his teeth.

2. For each sentence, tell how the word *diving* is used (the part of speech).

a. The diving submarine moved silently.

b. Our submarine is diving now.

c. Diving is easy for a submarine.

3. What is the meaning of the sentence?

The captain gave a tongue-lashing to the crew member who made the mistake.

4. A brochure that explains the features and performance of a new submarine is

○ expository writing ○ persuasive writing

○ narrative writing ○ imaginative writing

5. Number the steps sequentially for making a ship in a bottle.

___ During assembly, attach threads to the masts and roll up the sails.

___ When the ship is inside, pull the threads to raise the masts upright and unroll the sails.

___ Finally, use a wire with a dot of glue to secure the sails in place and to attach fittings to the ship.

___ Assemble the ship outside the bottle.

___ Slide the "folded" ship gently through the neck into the bottle.

___ To fit the ship in the bottle, fold the masts and remove the deck fittings.

___ First, put blue Plasticene into the bottle to resemble the "sea."

1. Write a homonym for each word.

serf   wade   sail

current   wave   wholly

2. Does the pronoun in this sentence agree with its antecedent?

The U.S.S. Whale is one of the submarines that gets their power from nuclear energy.

3. In which section of the Dewey Decimal system will you find reference books?

4. Write the present tense of each verb.

fought   went

took   lay

sat   sung

raised   left

You could call me the original spaceship.

5. Edit this selection.

A legendary ship it is at the center of a fascinating ghost story. The flying Dutchman is a phantom ship that was on a trip around Africas cape of good hope. According to the story, the tale says that the captain had a crew of dead men. Because of some curse on him or the ship The Dutchman sails forever never not reaching its port as it should of. This mysterious ship has become the subject of many pieces of literature and music, including Samuel Coleridges poem, The Rime of the Ancient Mariner.

Read

Countess LaMer has lost her priceless diamond somewhere on the yacht. Color or shade in each area described by these clues. Then, name the places where it might be found.

- It is not in the room below the Aft Deck.
- It is not in the room below the Galley.
- It is not on the Upper Bridge.
- It is not in the Master Stateroom or bathroom.
- It is not on the Flybridge Deck.
- It is not in the rooms below the Bridge.
- It is not in the bow of the boat.
- It is not in the Salon.

Where is the diamond?

THE SEA NYMPH
(Floor Plan)

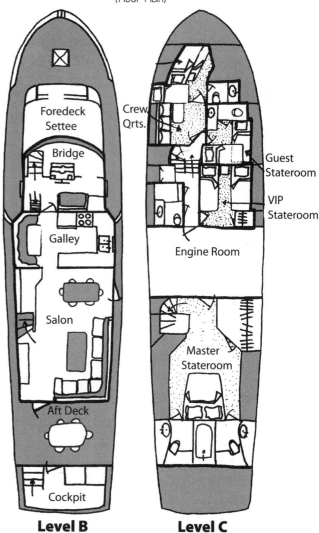

Foredeck Settee

Bridge

Crew Qrts.

Galley

Guest Stateroom

VIP Stateroom

Engine Room

Salon

Master Stateroom

Aft Deck

Cockpit

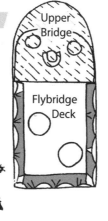

Upper Bridge

Flybridge Deck

Level A   **Level B**   **Level C**

Write

Write a smashing conclusion for a mystery about a stowaway on this yacht. The plot involves an anonymous tip radioed to the captain just after the yacht left port three days ago. The crew has been searching quietly for the stowaway so as not to alarm the countess.

Name

1. Edit the sentence.

The gulper eels tail is like a whip: it's mouth is wide and deep like a pelicans.

2. Choose the correct label for the sentence.

○ a fragment ○ run-on ○ complete

That ray, actually a flattened shark and harmless to humans.

3. What is the meaning of the underlined word?

Unlike some other sharks that tend to leave humans alone, the hammerhead can easily become an <u>assailant</u> to humans.

4. When the time comes to reproduce, every Pacific salmon remembers the smell of the stream in which it hatched, and it returns home. One sockeye salmon (a Pacific salmon) hatched last year in fresh water and migrated to the sea, where it lived for a year. Predict what will happen to this sockeye.

5. Which sentences contain metaphors?

a. The blue shark is a lightning bolt, streaking through blue water.

b. A masked villain, the lionhead fish swims stealthily among the weeds.

c. With its 20-foot wingspan, the manta is a dark, undulating saucer.

d. The viperfish moves with the motion of seaweed.

No, thank you. I've eaten.

Name

1. Circle the possessive pronouns.

mine   nobody   myself   theirs
who   ours   his   most

2. Rewrite the sentence with an active verb.

The sperm whale is a diver that can reach 10,000 feet below the surface.

3. Which words would be on a dictionary page with the guidewords **swordfish** and **synonym**?

○ swirl   ○ swordplay ○ synonym ○ system
○ sworn   ○ syllable   ○ swizzle   ○ symptom

4. Write the contractions.

would + not = _____

it + will = _____

we + are = _____

could + have = _____

5. Play this game with compound words. In each box, write a word that finishes a compound for the previous word and begins a compound for the word to follow.

A. cat [   ] hook

B. pop [   ] meal

C. inch [   ] hole

D. skate [   ] walk

E. match [   ] car

F. letter [   ] phones

En garde!

1. Capitalize this story title correctly.

I was slimed by an atlantic hagfish

2. What can you infer about the person who wrote the story in question one?

3. Which is **not** an antonym for **folly**?

○ sanity   ○ prudence

○ irrationality   ○ wisdom

4. Circle a participial phrase. Underline a prepositional phrase.

The pompon fish, looking fierce, shows fleshy "eyebrows" that grow from his nostrils.

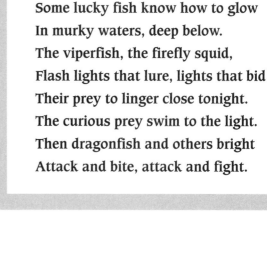

Go, Pompons! Go, team, go!

5. Identify the rhyming pattern in the poem. (Use letters such as a, b, c, d, etc., to describe the pattern.)

Some lucky fish know how to glow
In murky waters, deep below.
The viperfish, the firefly squid,
Flash lights that lure, lights that bid
Their prey to linger close tonight.
The curious prey swim to the light.
Then dragonfish and others bright
Attack and bite, attack and fight.

---

1. Correct the usage mistake.

Of all animals on Earth, the blue whale are the largest.

2. Edit the passage.

The longest fish migration on record was a trip by a blue fin tuna the fish traveled 5800 miles from Baja California Mexico to the sea south of Tokyo Japan

3. Finish the analogy:

_____ : dislocation :: migrate : immigration

4. What key word or phrase would be best for an encyclopedia search on information about poisonous ocean fish?

Glub.

5. Revise the passage so that it flows more smoothly and has a variety of sentence structures.

Just like other animals, fish need oxygen to stay alive. They get the oxygen they need from water. This can happen because fish have features called gills. Water flows into their mouths. It passes over the gills. The gills have tissue called lamellae tissue. Blood flows through these tissues. The blood absorbs oxygen from the water. The blood carries oxygen to all the fish's cells. The water then flows out of the fish through the gill openings on the sides of the fish's head.

Name

Read

1. What is the purpose of this writing selection?
2. Which frame of the cartoon contains a pun?
3. What is the meaning of the fish's exclamation in frame 2?
4. What is the meaning of the word **ingest** (frame 3)?
5. What is the meaning of the fish's warning in frame 3?

Fish at School *by Gil Minnoh*

Write

Rewrite each sentence below to clarify the meaning.

1. The fire on the beach looked good, being cold and weary from a long day of fishing.
2. Todd saw a swordfish loaded up with his gear getting onto the boat.
3. Bob and his fishing buddies heard about a storm coming on the radio.
4. I settled into a comfortable spot and caught a fish using my new pole.
5. The proud fishermen served the catch to their wives smothered in onions.
6. The green fisherman's vest fell off the pier.
7. After the fishing trip, we had our friend Joe for dinner.
8. While relaxing in my boat, several fish jumped at least a foot.

1. Add correct punctuation.

Is it true that more movies are made in India than in any other country

2. Choose the literary technique used in the sentence.

○ personification   ○ alliteration   ○ metaphor
○ hyperbole   ○ idiom   ○ simile

When I get to the movie store, my money knocks and claws at my pocket, begging to come out and hop up on the counter.

3. What is the meaning of the underlined word?

Al has such an <u>aversion</u> to animated films that he will never go to one again.

4. Write the plural form of each noun.

stereo patch   mouthful ax
theater belief clothes   crisis

I never tire of watching a good movie.

5. a. What is unique about the earnings of *Finding Nemo*?

   b. About how much did the movie earn after its first weekend?

The delightful animated film *Finding Nemo* was released on May 30, 2003. It earned $70,251,710 on the first weekend. Within one month, the earnings had jumped to $256 million. This movie about sea creatures surpassed *The Lion King, Tarzan*, and other successful titles to break all earnings records for animated films. By 2005, *Finding Nemo* had earned $850 million.

1. What kind of information can be found in the reference, *Bartlett's Familiar Quotations*?

2. Circle the silent letters.

**heirloom   muscle   thyme
gnash   pledge   balmy**

3. Circle the most precise word.

Georgio goes to eight movies a week. His mom, who is terribly worried, thinks his movie-going is (overdone, inordinate, frequent, consistent).

4. Circle suffixes meaning *one who*.

**producer   resident
adulthood   actor
occupant   childlike
scholar   artist**

I like to watch corny movies.

5. Each example contains a phrase. Label it **I** for infinitive; **G** for gerund, **PR** for prepositional, and **PA** for participial.

_____ a. Movie-watching is her favorite pastime.

_____ b. We waited for our popcorn.

_____ c. She couldn't wait to see Batman.

_____ d. Her least favorite activity is standing in line.

_____ e. Have you seen that actor performing in other movies?

1. Circle the correct word.

I (**assure, insure, ensure**) you that the smallest public theater in the world has only 21 seats.

2. Which sentence shows correct usage?

a. Jack Nicholson is the actor whom was nominated 12 times for an Oscar.

b. Who's the actress that won in 2004?

3. Correct the misspelled words.

outragious   anonamus

gorgous   jealuous

dangerus   suspiceous

4. Which literary technique is used?

Viewers love the screeches and scrapes, the pops and splatters, the smashes and crashes of those movie car chases.

See you at the movies.

5. Label each statement as fact (**F**) or opinion (**O**).

____ a. The first Spiderman movie earned $100 million in three days.

____ b. The first Spiderman movie was better than the second one.

____ c. Peter O'Toole deserved an Oscar but never won the award.

____ d. *The Lord of the Rings: The Return of the King* earned $1 billion in 11 weeks.

____ e. Producers of the movie *Chicken Run* used 5,240 pounds of Plasticine to make the movie.

1. Circle a proper adjective.

The movie *Zorro* featured Spanish-speaking heroes.

2. Choose the pair of synonyms.

○ contrive – scheme   ○ adept – skilled

○ obtuse – sharp   ○ laxity – looseness

3. Identify the verb tense.

Vic Armstrong began working as a movie stuntman at age 17.

4. Edit the sentence.

pirates of the caribbean: the curse of the black pearl* is the top-earning Pirate Film. This followed other popular Pirate movies such as *hook peter pan* and *shipwrecked

5. Are these fiction books stacked (top to bottom) in the order in which they would be found on a library shelf?

There's nothing better than a good book about movies.

THE POPCORN MYSTERY   KURNAL

LOST IN HOLLYWOOD   MCFINE

THE LAST MOVIE   NUMORE

A PARROT WITHOUT A PIRATE   POLLIE

THE FREEWAY PHANTOM   SPECTER

Read

Read each caption describing the movie characters. (The captions are below the blank frames.)
Draw the character that you imagine after reading the description.

THE BEACH CREATURE MOVIE, *Starring:*

I love to read about myself.

FAN-ZINE

Demi Devine *as Tiffany*
_____
_____
_____
_____
_____

Vern Vaign *as the Boyfriend*

The boyfriend thinks only about himself. He spends his time building his muscles, improving his tan, and strutting down the beach. He looks in the mirror quite often.

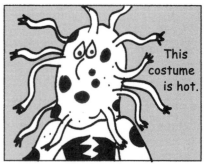

This costume is hot.

Sid Blotz *as the Creature*
_____
_____
_____
_____
_____

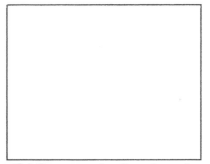

Ed Easy *as the Beachcomber*

What a laid-back guy—comfortable, tolerant, and relaxed! He stops and chats with everyone on the beach. When he's not snoozing or eating on the beach, he's combing it for lost stuff. It's amazing what he finds!

Heh, heh. I let the air out of the little kid's inner tubes.

Red Blaze *as the Bad Guy*
_____
_____
_____
_____
_____

Maya Maria *as Tootsie*

She looks small and shy, but watch out! She's a dynamite surfer. You should see her ride those waves. And Tootsie is a bit mysterious, too. You never know what she's up to.

Write

"Read" each picture to get a feel for the character. Then write a description of the character.

1. Circle the conjunction.

Warm air has less pressure than cool air because it is less dense.

2. Which word does not belong?

○ uniform   ○ monotone   ○ octopus

○ quadruped   ○ duet   ○ tripod

○ centennial   ○ airborne   ○ biannual

3. Which literary technique is used here?

Lacy claims that her antique replica of the Hindenburg blimp is an "air"-loom.

   a. consonance   c. imagery

   b. hyperbole   d. pun

4. Choose the examples with correct hyphen use.

○ two-thirds   ○ son-in-law   ○ vice-president

○ non-sense   ○ forty-two   ○ super-sonic

5. What is the main idea?

When a full balloon is not tied shut, it takes off like a jet as soon as you let go. There's a good explanation for that. When you blow up a balloon, the air pushes against the sides, and the sides (due to outside air pressure) push against the air inside. If the end is not pinched tightly, the air outside pushes the sides and squeezes the inside air. This forces the air out the opening and—*whoosh*—the balloon is propelled forward.

I'm full of hot air. Thank goodness.

1. Correct the sentence.

This airplane doesn't hardly have no space between the seats.

No room for passengers here.

2. Correct the spelling.

atmasphere   molacules   propell

barameter   seperate   flighte

3. One word is used twice. Give both meanings of the word.

Did your local TV station air the program about the hot-air balloon race?

4. Put these words in alphabetical order.

____ airport

____ airplane

____ aerial

____ aerodynamic

____ airline

5. What can you conclude about the power that is needed to launch and maneuver a space shuttle?

Two large booster rockets help to lift a space shuttle off the ground. Two minutes after the launch, these separate and parachute to earth, to be used again. Three main engines on the rear of the shuttle continue to push it forward. About ten minutes into the flight, two orbital maneuvering engines push the craft into orbit. The nose of the craft has 16 forward jet engines. These work with the rear engines to change directions once the craft is in space.

Name

1. Choose the correct word to complete the analogy.

impede : promote :: reprove : _____

○ rebuke   ○ praise   ○ reenact   ○ impair

2. Circle the action verb(s). Draw a box around the linking verb(s).

Over 3.5 million planes take off or land at Chicago's O'Hare Airport each year. That is about one plane every 45 seconds.

3. John pours a cup of boiling water into a tin can and immediately screws the top on tightly. As the air and water cool, the can collapses. What is probably the cause?

4. Rewrite this as a sentence with a quotation.

Britta told me that London's Heathrow Airport is the busiest international airport in the world.

5. Which selections would be examples of narrative writing?

    a. **a myth about birds with human capabilities**

    b. **a manual on how to fly a helicopter**

    c. **a travel brochure advertising a trip on a supersonic jet**

    d. **a science-fiction tale about time-traveling helicopters**

Where can I find a copy of that book?

Name

1. What is the meaning of the underlined word?

Before she began hang gliding, Jordan did plenty of research to <u>discern</u> the safest way to approach the sport.

2. Correct any misspelled words.

concieted   counterfeit   shiek

3. Circle the appositive.

We watched parachutes carrying two boosters, the rockets that launch the space shuttle.

4. Underline the topic sentence in question five.

Wow!

Bicycles can fly?

5. What does this encyclopedia entry tell about how the rider in the aircraft is protected from the wind?

Gossamer Albatross — It looks like a bicycle with wings, and in essence, it is. The Gossamer Albatross is a special aircraft built to be powered by human muscles. A bicycle is enclosed inside a thin shell to protect it from the wind. Attached to this "cage" are a long, narrow wing, a propeller on the back, and a small control wing. British biologist Bryan Allen pedaled the 75-pound craft across the English Channel in 1979.

Read

1. Gather these supplies:
- 8½ x 11 inch paper
- glue stick
- markers

2. Read and follow the directions.

Write

Fly your plane several times to become familiar with its behavior and *personality*!

1. Give your airplane a name. Write the name on the plane in colorful, interesting letters.

2. Decorate your plane with wonderfully descriptive words and phrases.

a. Write 10 words that describe its look, shape, feel, "personality," or sound.

b. Write 10 verbs that describe its actions and movements.

c. Write some similes and comparisons, such as

as sleek as . . .

Its shape is as . . . as . . .

wings are like . . .

floats like . . .

sounds like . . .

funnier than . . .

swift as . . .

tumbles faster than . . .

cuts through air like . . .

Its nose is as . . . as . . .

It dips and dives as . . . as . . .

I'd rather fly my airplane than . . .

SWOOP...SWISH!

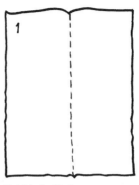
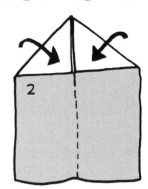

Fold in half. Open. Turn over.

Fold corners to the center.

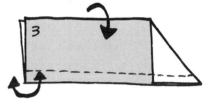

Fold in half, flap side out. Draw a line one inch from bottom.

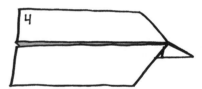

Fold flaps down at the line, to match figure #4.

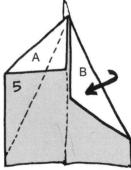

Turn plane over and fold wings into the center. See part A and B of figure #5.

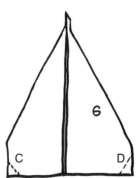

Turn plane over. It should look like figure #6. Fold wing tips up at C and D.

Glue center together for extra stability. Fly!

1. Insert correct punctuation in the box.

Armor was expensive ☐ therefore, only wealthy men became knights.

2. What kind of sentence?
    a. simple   c. compound
    b. complex   d. compound-complex

With 4,200 royal princes and 40,000 other relatives, the Saudi royal family is the largest in the world.

3. Give an antonym for **contiguous**.

4. A story is told by a prince who is a character in the story. The point of view is
    a. first person
    b. second person
    c. third person

Uh, oh!

I'm rusted stiff!

5. In Britain, the eldest son of the reigning monarch is next in line for the throne. The line of succession then follows to his children. After that, the line goes to the second son and his children. The successions continue through all the siblings, sons first. A daughter can inherit the throne if there are no sons.

Today, Queen Elizabeth II reigns in England. If her eldest son, his children, and her second eldest son were not able or willing to take the position, who would be the next heir to the throne?

1. Does the pronoun agree with its antecedent?

Every one of the queen bee's workers spend their lives feeding the queen.

2. The queen bee has a **penchant** for honey. What does this mean?

3. Correct any misspelled words.

braid   dred   coughing

applawd   nurotic   broyle

4. Edit the sentence.

Her majesty queen Elizabeth ii ascendedto the throne on february 6 1952 upon the death of her father king george vi.

The buzz is all about the honey.

5. A dictionary lists these meanings for a word. What is the word?

- **something that makes vision possible *n.***
- **a source of illumination *n.***
- **to make bright *v.***
- **to set on fire *v.***
- **having little weight *adj.***
- **exerting a minimum of force *adj.***
- **pale in color *adj.***

Name

What do I know? I'm only a pawn.

1. Give the part of speech for each underlined word.

According to the <u>legend</u>, King Arthur <u>fought</u> <u>valiantly</u> in the battle <u>against</u> the intruders.

2. Circle the correct word for the sentence.

Lucy gained (**notary, notoriety**) for her ability to capture other players' knights in the game of chess.

3. Circle letters that should be capitals.

she plays chess every day of the year except sundays, st. patrick's day, easter, bastille day, and thanksgiving.

4. What is the meaning of this sentence?

The queen went out on a limb to bestow knighthood on me.

I knighted Sir Gallops-a-lot at night.

Thank you.

5. From the information given in the passage, what can you conclude about the truth of the Arthur legends?

Was there a real King Arthur? Historians agree that there probably was (back in the 500s), but little is known about him. Most of the stories of his adventures are legends. As popular as they are, they may not be true. The stories are of a great warrior who pulled a magic sword, Excalibur, from a block of stone to prove himself the rightful heir to the throne. He married Princess Guinevere and lived in his favorite castle, Camelot. Arthur supposedly gathered a group of the best knights (the Knights of the Round Table), who accomplished many brave deeds.

Name

1. Write a homonym for each of three words in this sentence.

Did the king just hear that a rival knight is about to seize the kingdom?

King me!

2. Write the plural of each noun.

victory   clash   sword

grandchild   horse   castle

3. Revise the sentence for clear meaning.

The queen rode in a carriage adorned in the finest gold crown and velvet robe.

4. Describe three kinds of information about words that can be found in a dictionary.

5. How long did Liliuokalani reign?

Aloha, faithful subjects.

When Hawaiian King Kalakaua died in 1891, his sister Liliuokalani took the throne. As queen, she tried to change the laws to give herself more power. In 1893, a small group revolted and removed her from power, ending the monarchy in Hawaii.

Read

1. Use the information from the table to complete a bar graph.
2. Which queen had the longest reign (other than the queen still on the throne)?
3. How long was the reign of the queen from Italy?

Name	Country	Years of Reign
Queen Suiko Tenno	Japan	593-628
Queen Wu Chao	China	655-705
Queen Joanna I	Italy	1343-1381
Queen Elizabeth I	United Kingdom	1558-1603
Queen Maria Theresa	Hungary	1740-1780
Queen Maria I	Portugal	1776-1816
Queen Isabella II	Spain	1833-1868
Queen Victoria	United Kingdom	1837-1901
Queen Wilhelmina	Netherlands	1890-1948
Queen Elizabeth II	United Kingdom	1952-present

THE WORLD'S LONGEST REIGNING QUEENS

REIGN, IN YEARS	30	35	40	45	50	55	60	65	70
THE QUEENS									

CHECK this out, MATE.

You win again, Queenie.

Write

Write a paragraph explaining why you would (or would not) want to be a queen (or a king). Give at least three clear details or examples to support your position.

1. What is the meaning of all the root words?

invisible	video	spectator
revise	visual	scrutinize

2. Which sentence has a predicate noun?

a. Van Gogh's paintings are marvelous!

b. Van Gogh is a master!

3. Circle the correctly spelled words.

innocence   resistence

nuisence   persistence

4. A flier is sent to a mailing list of art students. It advertises an art fair and offers big discounts on artwork. What kind of writing is this?

○ imaginative   ○ expository

○ persuasive   ○ narrative

Do you think I'll have a career as an artist?

5. Which work of art would you most like to see? Tell why.

- The world's longest painting— of 1,500 horses, 6,600 feet
- The world's largest painting— a painting of the sea, 92,419 sq ft
- The world's tallest freestanding sculpture—Chief Crazy Horse, 563 ft
- The largest cardboard-box sculpture—a red Ford Torino car, 88 x 23 x 7 ft
- The longest drawing done by 2,000 children—"My World," 4,068 ft
- The most valuable Old Master painting—a work by Peter Paul Rubens, $76.7 million

1. Are pronouns used correctly?

She and I went to Barcelona to see Gaudi's unusual architecture.

2. Give the meaning of **conscientious**.

3. Insert commas in the correct places.

Claude Monet the great impressionist painter was born in Paris France on November 14 1840.

4. Alphabetize these artists' names.

Edgar Degas	Pablo Picasso
Salvador Dali	Andrew Wyeth
Vincent Van Gogh	Claude Monet

I have many talents.

5. Write a paragraph about Jim Davis. Use the topic sentence and include at least three details.

Jim Davis, the creator of the cartoon *Garfield*, grew up on a farm with plenty of cats.

- **His knowledge of animals helped him draw cartoon cats and dogs.**
- **Garfield is a fat, lazy, cynical, lasagna-loving cat.**
- **The Garfield cartoon debuted in 41 newspapers in 1978.**
- **Today, it is in 2,600 papers, reaching 263 million readers.**

1. Correct the misspelled words.

exagerate   excperation   excusses

exeption   exxcess   complextion

2. Which word does not belong?

○ elude   ○ exclude   ○ escape   ○ avoid

3. Circle the demonstrative pronoun(s).

Those big paintings in the library are mine; they are the most expensive ones in that room.

4. Which examples include **alliteration**?

    a. Gold spikes shoot across the canvas.

    b. Mellow green paint looks like new grass.

    c. Painters patiently prepare pallets.

    d. Soft stripes of silver shimmer.

I'm pretty enough to hang on the wall.

Hmmm, she might be right.

5. What conclusion can you draw about the experience of the painters?

Art Sold At Lapp School Art Auction

Artist	Painting Title	Selling Price
J. Bledsoe	Evening Visitor	$12
K. Mack	Karla's Carousel	$42
A. Anan	Sunburst	$36
P. Ramon	Dreamscape	$28
R. Malari	Lost	$44
C. Thomas	Forest Fire	$19

---

1. Shaun checks out a book that has pictures and descriptions of Renaissance paintings. It is probably

○ fiction   ○ nonfiction   ○ biography

2. What is the meaning of this sentence?

That new sculpture of Professor Frank's cost him an arm and a leg.

I really like my new look.

3. Edit the sentence.

It took 25297 painters three years two months to complete the painting A Little Dab of Texas.

4. Circle the direct object(s).

The largest inflatable sculpture in the world boasts a blockhead and a huge nose.

5. Write a conclusion for this article. Then give it a good title.

_____

This news from the art world is sure to surprise you. A very young artist named Dante Lam has had his work chosen for hanging in a Georgia gallery. Last week, one of his paintings sold for $85. What is amazing is that this painter is three years old.

_____

_____

_____

Name

Read

This passage is an example of "painted" writing—writing that looks like art. The words are written on the page in a manner that suggests the subject of the passage.

1. What genre (kind) of writing is this?
2. Circle any similes.
3. Underline an example of personification.
4. Put a star by lines with alliteration.
5. Put an X after lines that contain onomatopoeia.

The fireworks have begun their show.
So catch your breath and hold your ears.
Drops of turquoise give the night a fresh shower
And pretty-patterned purples paint a dark canvas.
Sharp crimson spikes shoot like arrows.
Glistening golds scatter glitter
While blasts of blues burst into the blackness.
Fuscia fragments fling themselves,
Chasing after twinkling chartreuse puff-balls.
Yellows sparkle, stretching their wiggly fingers out
To claw at the skies.
The silence is split by cracks and pops.
Confetti explosions roar and clatter,
Shattering the night.

BOOM crackle... Pop!

Write

Write your own "painted" poem or sentence. Choose a subject that lends itself to a visual approach. Write the passage. Then use good-sized, readable letters to print the passage on paper in a shape that will instantly give the reader a "feeling" of the topic. Here are a few ideas:

flying bird	ocean wave	lightning	bouncing ball	cyclone
footsteps	speeding train	wind	rainbow	fire
sandwich	climbing stairs	octopus	roller coaster	pretzel

1. Does this show the correct use of the dash?

> **Believe it or not—Jim Purol can stuff 151 drinking straws into his mouth at one time!**

2. Give the meaning of each prefix.

inconceivable   hypersensitive   retroactive

3. Rewrite the sentence in future tense.

> **H.C. Harris whistles at the same time that he plays a harmonica with his nose.**

4. Identify the bias of the poem in question five.

I wouldn't have believed it if I hadn't read it here.

> *Dr. Vargas should have stayed To be the president. Three times elected, he said, "No!" Then packed his stuff and went.*

5. Describe similarities and differences in the two passages.

> Listen to this unusual story of a man who could have been president of his country, but refused. Doctor Jose Maria Vargas was elected three times to be president of Venezuela. But, he did not want to be president. So each time, he refused. Finally, to get away from the pressure to take the leadership, he fled from Venezuela.

1. Circle the words that are always capitalized.

european	**mother**	**president**
chicago	**halloween**	**antarctica**

2. Choose the correct word for the sentence.

> **In Belgium, a musician performed a concert for a herd of 3,000 (diary, dairy) cows.**

3. The denotations of **grab** and **seize** are similar. Explain how their connotations are different.

4. On which dictionary page would **credible** be found?

cramp	**109**	creak
cream	**110**	creepy
cremate	**111**	crypt

5. Edit the passage.

> ### Believe it Or not!
>
> When a woman from collingwood australia lost her voice for a long time she hopped it wuld return. But she nevver imagind how it would return! An accadent cauzed the loss of ellen Matthers voice. Seven and one half years later her voice returnd with a scottish accent. She was Australian, not Scottish!

Get that woman a bagpipe.

1. Insert an apostrophe correctly.

We cheered Mat Pendls ability to spin 30 hula hoops at the same time.

2. What is the meaning of **preposterous**?

3. Circle the preposition(s).
Underline the prepositional phrase(s).

The daily requirement of some important minerals (calcium, phosphorous, iron) can be fulfilled by eating 20 caterpillars.

4. What is the rhyming pattern of the poem?
In northern Alaska, when nights are cold
And the temperature below zero falls,
Eggs left outdoors get frozen so well
That they can bounce like rubber balls.

5. Write a brief summary of the passage.

In 1919, a heavy storm with wild seas brought disaster to the S.S. Ethie steamer. It was breaking apart in the high waves. The winds were so strong that a crew could not get a lifeline to the shore to stabilize the lifeboats. All the passengers on board would perish without a lifeline. But there was hope! A dog was able to make the swim with the line. All 92 passengers were able to use the lifeline to be pulled to safety.

A St. Bernard has a cask; a sea dog has a lifeline.

1. Correct the misspelled words.
jealousey   theory   signify   simptoms

2. Choose the pairs that are not antonyms.
○ averse – supportive
○ significant – trivial
○ reject – repudiate
○ deceit – treachery

3. Circle an independent clause.

A company in Japan produces false fingernails that glow in the dark when a person is using a cell phone.

4. What information can be found on the title page of a book?

After thirty years, some of us are a little out of style.

5. Choose the most precise word to complete the sentence.
○ interesting   ○ sobering
○ amusing   ○ annoying
○ curious   ○ convenient

For people in America who enjoy the multiple phones in their homes and easy access to cell phones, it might be _____ to learn that there are places in Africa where people have to wait 30 years for a phone to be installed in their home.

Read

Read these headlines about real-life happenings, as cited in the 2002 edition of
Ripley's Believe-It-Or-Not: Encyclopedia of the Bizarre.

1. What theme do the bathtub, dog, and cyclones headlines have in common?

2. Which story seems to involve the greatest number of people?

3. Write the numeral associated with the worm headline.

4. Why might the word **chocolate** be in quotation marks?

5. Which story sounds the most outrageous to you?

"Chocolate" Snow Falls in July

9-Year-Old Boy Rides Out Flood in Bathtub

Ten Couples Married Simultaneously on a Ferris Wheel

Newfoundland Dog Saves 92 Shipwrecked Passengers

Man Wins Truck By Diving For Keys in Green Jello

NEW YORK WOMAN WILLS $30 MILLION TO POODLE

Cyclone Carries Illinois Girl 8 Miles in Her Bed

Two Hundred Fifty Billion Worms Perish in Holland Flood

Write

Choose one of these unbelievable events. Pretend that you are somehow in or connected to the story. Write a letter to a good friend, telling all about what happened and what part you had in it. Follow the correct form of a friendly letter.

1. Circle the silent letters.

A quiet spider wraps its prey in silky threads, then calmly fastens a chord of silk to the ledge and speedily climbs down to the floor.

2. Create ten compound words that have **head** as the first or last part of the new word.

_____head	head_____
_____head	head_____
_____head	head_____
_____head	head_____
_____head	head_____

3. Circle the adjectives.

Every single spider — from the tiny armored spider to the giant tarantula — is lucky enough to have eight legs.

4. What is the myth's theme in question five?

I'm just hanging around.

5. Summarize this passage.

The tale of young Arachne is an ancient Greek myth written by the poet Ovid. Arachne was a young woman who bragged that she could weave as well as the goddess Athena. The two held a contest, and Arachne was the loser. She tried to hang herself in shame and fear. At this moment, the goddess punished her by changing her into a spider. According to the story, Arachne and her descendents have been spiders ever since then— weavers that hang from a thread.

1. Finish the sentence with an infinitive phrase.

When Andy looked up and saw the huge spider above him, his first instinct was . . .

2. What is the meaning of the underlined word?

Suzie <u>feigned</u> disinterest in the scorpion crawling toward her, but we could tell she was watching the insect closely.

3. Write a topic sentence to begin a story about a person who trains tarantulas to perform tricks.

Do you think I should shave my legs?

4. Insert parentheses correctly.

Australia's most famous poisonous spider the Sydney funnel-web spider has not caused any deaths in recent years.

5. Predict what would happen to a teenager stung by a scorpion.

Scorpion — A scorpion is an insect with a stinging tail. The animal belongs to the arachnid class, all members of which have eight appendages. The first pair is tiny pincers; the second pair is large claws. The other four appendages are legs. A scorpion has 6 to 12 eyes, depending on the species. The stinger is a curved organ at the end of the powerful tail. This contains glands that give out poison. It is painful to be stung by a scorpion, but the wound rarely causes death.

1. A recluse brown spider carries deadly venom. Is it **caustic** or **toxic**?

2. Circle the indefinite pronouns.

anybody	theirs	some	mine
several	either	all	none

3. Circle the correctly-spelled words.

dangerous	instead	measurment
polatics	nervus	regonize

4. What is the purpose of this example?

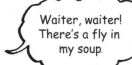

Waiter, waiter! There's a fly in my soup.

Don't worry, Sir. The spider in your salad will catch it.

5. Make an inference about why many people are quick to kill spiders.

There are 37,000 different species of spiders. Very few of these (only about 35) have venom that has any effect on humans. There are only two species in the United States that have been known to cause deaths: the black widow and the brown recluse. Yet most people, upon spotting a leggy, scampering spider, will immediately swat it or step on it. (That is, unless they are too frightened to do even that.)

1. Give the meaning for each different use of the word **count**.

I watched you count the spiders you caught in the contest. You cheated, so your score doesn't count.

2. Make corrections in the usage.

Anyways, how come the black widow female she eats the male after mating? Is it because he snores so bad?

3. Choose the one(s) that may be found on the Internet?

○ today's weather   ○ history of silk farms

○ yesterday's news   ○ a definition of arachnid

4. Revise the sentence to give it more action.

The Goliath birdeater tarantula is big and strong enough to snatch a bird out of its nest.

5. Add correct punctuation and capitalization to this business letter.

Professor J. mite
Department of zoology
Chicago university
chicago IL 60606

april 4 2005

dear professor mite
I would like to take a course that studies arachnids. Can you make a suggestion of where I might find such a course

yours truly
Chester C. webbs

Read

Read the conversations between two friends trapped in a dark room full of spiders.

1. Why do spiders carry venom?

2. Which friend is most afraid of spiders?

3. What is the meaning of the word **conjecture** in the third frame?

4. What information about spiders is given in this cartoon?

5. Circle the sentences that are exclamatory.

Fred, spiders carry venom to stun their prey, not to harm humans. Only 35 species are harmful to humans.

That's 35 too many! I have arachnophobia.

A Goliath tarantula can be as big as 12 inches wide.

Ted, I am sorry you told me that.

The light is dim, but I'm going to offer a conjecture that the thing on your shoulder is a black widow.

E-E-E-E-E-E-EK!

Write

Rewrite each conversation using dialogue. Capitalize and punctuate the conversation correctly.

1._____

_____

_____

2._____

_____

_____

3_____

_____

_____

1. Insert commas in the correct places.

   On a trip to see some of the biggest swamps in the United States Sophie saw the Dismal Swamp the Okefenokee Swamp and the Everglades.

2. Finish the analogy.

   swamp : alligator :: _____ : reindeer

3. Write the singular form of each noun.

   vetoes   teeth   measles   oxen

   watches   cacti   wolves   pennies

4. Which word best describes the mood of the passage in question five?

   a. futility   c. optimism

   b. suspicion   d. anger

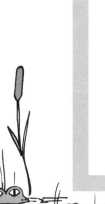

5. What factors have led to the deterioration of the Everglades?

The plight of the Everglades Swamp is dismal indeed. Even with many efforts by environmentalists to protect the area, the condition of this wetland area is deteriorating. Widespread development has decreased the size of the swamp and brought much toxic pollution to the area. A project to straighten the Kissimmee River has significantly reduced the flow of water into the swamp. Together, these factors have jeopardized the health of plant and animal life in the swamp. These are major problems that are not easy to remedy.

1. Circle the adverbs in the sentence.

   Is that a scaly crocodile lazily raising his narrow snout out of the brackish water?

2. Correct the misspelled words.

   Southren Flordia is the only place in the world were allagators and crocadiles share the same habatat.

3. For each meaning, write a word with a prefix.

   not normal   spend too much

4. This book is probably

   ○ fiction

   ○ nonfiction

   ○ biography

Alligators
I Have
Wrestled

Ima Tuffwon

5. Write a brief description to accompany this scene.

WEDNESDAY WEEK 24 _____ LANGUAGE PRACTICE

1. Identify the technique(s) used in the description.

An alligator-wrestling match is a lot of grunts, shouts, and yelps mixed with gnashing, splashing, and crunching.

○ rhythm   ○ onomatopoeia

○ hyperbole   ○ alliteration

○ simile   ○ metaphor

2. What is the meaning of **perilous**?

3. Punctuate and capitalize this article title.

how to get out of an alligators grip

4. Correct the usage mistakes.

How come you're taking a trip to the Dismal Swamp? You will sure put yourself into danger unnecessarily.

5. Follow the directions to finish the drawing of the alligator.

1. Add eyes that sit up on top of the head.
2. Draw scales all the way down the back and tail.
3. Draw six upper teeth coming out of the mouth.
4. Color the animal a dark grey-green.

THURSDAY WEEK 24 _____ LANGUAGE PRACTICE

1. Explain the meaning of the sentence.

Seventy-one-year-old George Blenin was in a pretty pickle when he fell off a dock into the jaws of an alligator.

2. Correct any misspelled words.

Snackes, oppossums, foxs, and bares all live in the Dismal Swampp of North Carilina and Virginnia.

Help!

3. Write a possessive phrase that means

a. the jaws of a crocodile

b. the bites of three alligators

4. Correct the usage errors.

This here alligator has a broad snout and several upper teeth that shows.

5. Rewrite each sentence with an active verb.

a. Which crocodile is snapping his jaws?

b. Mort is wrestling an alligator.

c. Three angry crocs seem to be after your boat.

d. That one looks able to devour your arm in a minute.

75

Use It! Don't Lose It! IP 612-2

Read

1. What is the tone of these selections?
2. How are the selections alike?
3. What audience(s) might find these passages interesting or enjoyable?
4. What is the meaning of the word **endeavoring** in the first passage?
5. What is the meaning of the word **substantially** in the second passage?

How To Prevent Alligator Bites

The best prevention is endeavoring to avoid alligators at all costs. If you find yourself in a relationship with an alligator, get a suit made of metal or six-inch thick rubber. (You can even wear five wet suits on top of each other.) These materials are too hard or thick for the teeth to penetrate. When you get close to the alligator, offer him (or her) a bag of rippled potato chips and some salsa before you begin any interaction. It is best if the chips have extra salt.

CURE FOR ALLIGATOR BITES

IF AN ALLIGATOR BITES YOU, ACT IMMEDIATELY TO MIX THIS POTION. MIX THE JUICE OF 12 LIMES WITH 2 CUPS OF COOKED SPINACH. STIR IN A CUP OF DRY OATMEAL AND A TABLESPOON OF MOTOR OIL. SPREAD THIS OVER THE AFFECTED AREA RIGHT AWAY. THEN COVER THE AREA WITH BANANA PEELS AND WRAP IT TIGHTLY IN PLASTIC WRAP. WAIT AN HOUR. THE BITE SHOULD BE SUBSTANTIALLY BETTER.

Write

Write a prevention or cure for any ailment of your choice. Here are some ideas:

warts	jealousy
broken heart	embarrassment
sore throat	indigestion
ringing ears	procrastination
nosebleeds	indecision
headaches	ingrown toenails
toothache	ears that stick out
acne	chicken pox

76

1. Choose the word that does not belong.

○ gnarled   ○ heiress   ○ rhinoceros

○ knuckle   ○ wrist   ○ panther

2. Give the part of speech for each underlined word.

A cave, <u>also</u> known as a cavern, <u>is</u> a naturally-occurring <u>hollow</u> in the earth large <u>enough</u> for a person to <u>enter</u>.

3. Correct the spelling errors.

You can be shure that itll be damp and dark in the caves interier. Walk carefuly, becuse it is sliperry and rocky.

4. What literary technique is used in this sentence?

The inside of that cavern is like the surface of another planet.

5. Circle the **cause** in each example.

    a. Most caves are formed by the action of underground water.

    b. The moving water dissolves some kinds of rock.

    c. Sea caves are formed when surf pounds on rocks along the shore and wears away the weakest rock.

    d. A sinkhole results when the roof of a cave collapses.

1. Write the correct form of the adjective **good** in the blank.

Responsible cavers want to leave each cave in the _____ condition possible.

2. What can be found in a book's glossary?

3. Edit the sentence.

Today, grandpa smith led a group of 20 german tourists on a tour of crystal cave.

4. Which words are synonyms for **explore**?

○ plumb   ○ probe   ○ implore

○ scrutinize   ○ elucidate   ○ divulge

Hmmm?

oceans
tides
pools
fish
hatcheries
lava
caves
digs

5. Add a missing detail.

Mrs. Bunson's seventh grade science class discussed ideas for their next field trip. The teacher said they could vote to choose the location. The ideas suggested included: ocean tide pools, an aquarium, caves, lava beds, or a fish hatchery.

Just five weeks later, the students tumbled out of the bus, laced up sturdy boots, put on their rain jackets, stuffed food into their pockets, tried out their headlamps, put on their helmets, and headed down into the caves.

1. Correct the mistakes in usage.

Brad and me explored all 12 miles of the public route in the Mammoth Caves Next time, you should come along with he and I!

2. Choose the words with a suffix meaning **resembling**.

○ falsehood   ○ childlike   ○ magical

○ angelic   ○ ageless   ○ clarify

3. Correct the misspelled words.

Several freinds and nieghbors took up the riskey hobbie of caving. They tried lots of eazy routes before takeing on a diffacult caving expidition.

4. Read the passage in question five. Make a prediction about the future of the business described by the poster.

5. What mode of literature is shown?

○ expository   ○ persuasive

○ narrative   ○ imaginative

Sassy Spelunkers
Cavetown, Kentucky

We'll Take You Caving
Sign up today!
No experience needed.
Go lightweight.

We won't burden you with...
*heavy boots, bulky clothes,
ugly helmets, awkward knee pads,
multiple lights, or restrictions.
Just enjoy leisurely strolls through
spectacular caverns.*

Call 332-1010

1. What kind of phrase is the underlined phrase?

<u>Hanging bats</u> populate most of the caves.

2. Make the sentence(s) complete.

Bats have a scary reputation they are not particularly harmful to humans however

3. Write a homonym for each of three words in the sentence.

Part of the cavers' motto is: Kill nothing but time. Do not even leave boot prints.

4. Capitalize the phrases correctly.

flint ridge cave

national park service

echo river

I'm looking for a new cave.

5. What is the largest river inside the cave system?

Mammoth Cave

I.   Location and size
    A. Central Kentucky
    B. Green and Nolan Rivers
    C. 144 miles long

II. Formation
    A. Formed in limestone ridge
    B. Acidic water seeped through cracks

III. Inside the cave
    A. Rock formations
    B. Echo River, the largest river
    C. Many rivers, lakes, waterfalls
    D. Fishes and bats

Name

Read

1. Which rules relate to things you should do before you enter the cave?

2. Describe the outfit you should wear.

3. Why does leaving the cave take longer than heading in?

4. Why might it be recommended that each caver carry three light sources?

Look, Betty, we have company...

SAFE CAVING GUIDELINES

1. Never cave alone. Plan to go with three or more people.

2. Let someone outside the cave know where and when you are going, and when you will return.

3. Check the weather before you go in. Make sure there is no danger of the cave flooding. (Avoid rainy days.)

4. Wear substantial clothing in layers. Your outer layer should be waterproof.

5. If you are going into caves with water, wear a wetsuit.

6. Wear sturdy shoes or boots.

7. Always carry food (sweets and some protein).

8. Take at least three long-lasting light sources.

9. Wear a helmet at all times.

10. Know the way out of the cave. As you go along, mark the return route. Take more time for your exit than your entrance. Remember that it is harder on the way out, since you'll be climbing up for your exit. Also, you will be tired at the end of your caving trip (and possibly cold and wet, too).

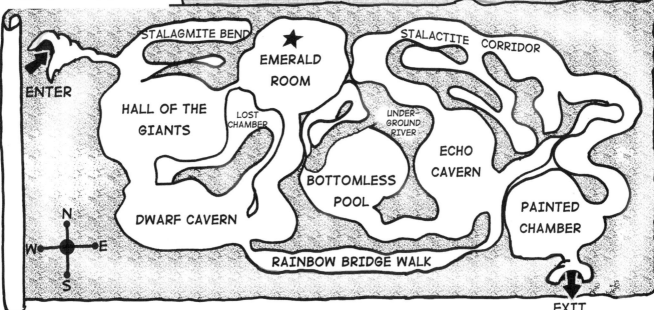

Write

Write clear instructions for getting out of the cave (from the star) to the exit.

1. Choose the correct word for each sentence.

   a. Harold Calvert is the man (**who, whom**) got a credit card for his dog, Ginger.

   b. (**Whose, Who's**) Ginger's owner?

   c. (**Whomever, Whoever**) would give a credit card to a dog?

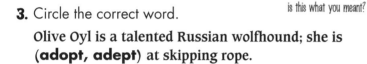

When you said, "Charge," - is this what you meant?

2. Add correct punctuation.

My question is this Who pays the dogs credit card bills

3. Circle the correct word.

Olive Oyl is a talented Russian wolfhound; she is (**adopt, adept**) at skipping rope.

4. Identify the setting of the selection in question five.

5. Write a summary of the passage.

A Search and Rescue Dog (SAR dog) has an amazing ability to track a person. Molly is one such dog. Her superior sense of smell, hearing, and sight helped her locate a little girl lost in a California forest. The dog was taken to the spot in the campground where Beth was last seen. Rescuers let Molly smell Beth's hat. Molly moved with her nose to the ground and followed the smell of Beth's skin cells along the path and on the bushes. This led her right to the spot where Beth was huddled, asleep, off the trail against a tree.

---

1. Add an –**ing** ending to each word.

regret   fuss   beg

hope   rob   supply

2. Circle the simple subject.

When the darkling beetle is threatened, he stands on his head and squirts out a bad-smelling liquid.

3. What key word would be best for an encyclopedia search on bombardier beetles in Africa?

  ○ Africa   ○ bombardier

  ○ beetle   ○ insects

4. Rewrite the instruction on this sign so that it uses an antonym to give the opposite message.

Do Not Placate the Animals

5. Edit the selection.

  • A flock of sparows, in New Zeeland, learned to open the autamatic doors of a buss station.

  • A dog named Brutus has a busy, skydiving career.

  • A Northern pine snake has the amasing ability to swallow, and breath at the same time.

  • An African grasshopper blows bitter, bad-smelling bubbels when danger is neer.

  • The bombardier beetle scalds its enemys by spraying boiling liquid.

Name

1. Capitalize and punctuate the sentence.

Did you know asked Luke that a longhorn bull named Merril was trained to star in a TV commercial

2. The bull was anything but nimble in that china shop. Was the bull less than **graceful** or less than **gracious**?

3. Which writing explains or informs?

○ narrative   ○ persuasive

○ descriptive   ○ expository

○ imaginary   ○ personal-expressive

4. Which includes a present tense verb?

     a. Merril starred in a movie.

     b. Merril will be a star.

     c. The bull is starring in a new movie.

5. Write your impressions about the personality and interests of the homeowner who has these lawn signs.

Name

1. Revise the sentence to be more active, colorful, and interesting.

Peppy, a Dalmatian, is able to roll a log a mile in just one hour.

2. Explain the two meanings of the word **spotted** used in the sentence.

Daphne is a spotted dog who spotted a runaway train a half-mile away.

3. Correct the misspelled words.

     peculier   origanal

     babboon   interupt

4. A dictionary entry for the word **star** has the symbol **v.** listed next to one definition and **n.** listed next to another. What do these symbols mean?

5. Which examples have linking verbs?

     a. Peppy is a Dalmatian.

     b. She has an amazing talent.

     c. Ginger charges dog food on a credit card.

     d. Merril the bull performs on TV.

     e. All these animals are amazing.

Halt!

Use It! Don't Lose It! IP 612-2

Read

1. How many of the descriptions include statistics?

2. Which of the animal feats probably involved some training?

3. Which animal feat is most fascinating to you? Why?

ANIMAL FEATS

Striker, a border collie, has an unusual talent. He can roll down a non-electric car window in 11.34 seconds. This is a world record, set in Canada in 2004.

Imagine a horse that makes predictions! In the 1940s, a horse named Lady Wonders predicted world events such as the reelection of President Truman. Even more amazing is this: the horse spelled out the predictions on a typewriter.

The midge is just a tiny insect, but it has the fastest muscle movement ever measured. This little bug can beat its wings 62,769 times a minute!

Five lucky ducks get an elevator ride every day. For the past 50 years, the ducks have ridden from their home on the roof of the Peabody Hotel down to the lobby to swim in the fountain. What luxury!

When the U.S. Space Command in Colorado needed some help getting into small spaces, they called on a ferret. The animal helped to rewire the computers in their command center.

A British animal-handler trained two elephants to eat like humans. They sat beside the table, ate food with forks, and finished dinner by drinking wine from goblets.

Write

1. Write a title for each description above.

2. Finish a couplet about each of the animal feats. (The lines in a couplet must rhyme.)

Whenever Striker rides to town
_____

Do you know elephants who are able
_____

A ferret sleek can squeeze through places
_____

The tiny midge's muscles strong
_____

Lady Wonder, that clever horse
_____

Quacks greet the elevator door
_____

1. Is this complete, run-on, or a fragment?

"Banana" George Blair, setting a world record as the oldest barefoot water skier.

2. Create six compound words that contain the word **foot**.

3. Write the past tense of each verb.

rise	think	buy	go
go	is	ring	lose

4. The angle or perspective from which the story is told is the

○ plot   ○ theme   ○ point of view

○ setting   ○ mood   ○ characterization

5. Which events took place about nine years apart?

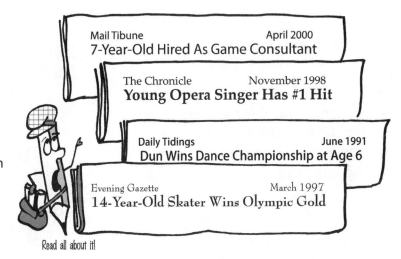

Mail Tibune   April 2000
7-Year-Old Hired As Game Consultant

The Chronicle   November 1998
Young Opera Singer Has #1 Hit

Daily Tidings   June 1991
Dun Wins Dance Championship at Age 6

Evening Gazette   March 1997
14-Year-Old Skater Wins Olympic Gold

Read all about it!

1. What does this sentence mean?

This biography of Paul McCartney is right up my alley.

He strikes just the right note.

2. Punctuate the sentence correctly.

Twelve-year old Jennifer Capriatis win of a Wimbledon tennis match changed everyones view of her.

3. Circle the dependent clause.

When he recorded his debut album, 12-year old Billy Gilman didn't expect to sell a million copies.

4. Are these words in alphabetical order?

biography, biannual, biodegradable, biped, bye, buyer, bygones

5. Eliminate any unnecessary words or phrases.

Amadeus Wolfgang Mozart was a prodigy, an unusually intelligent young person. At age five, Mozart he was composing music. By age 13, he was presenting concerts throughout Europe and had written several hard, difficult pieces of music, including symphonies. Although he is now regarded as one of the most important composers of greatest influence in history, he died in poverty as a poor man at age 35.

1. Give the meaning of the root of each word.

biography   automotive   inedible

2. Correct any misspelled words.

A man in South Afraca has doenated bloud for 59 conseckitive years,

3. Does the subject agree with the verb?

A group of reporters want to interview Microsoft owner, Bill Gates.

4. A well-known singer sits and reads to an audience something she has written that tells the details of the most important experience of her life.

This writing is

    a. narrative   c. persuasive

    b. expository   d. imaginary

5. Describe two similarities and two differences in the information gained about the two young people.

Tara Lipinski (USA) won an Olympic Gold medal for figure skating at the 1997 Winter Olympics. She was 14 years, 286 days old, and still holds the record as the youngest person to win this honor.

Andrew Cooney (United Kingdom) is the youngest person to walk from the edge of the Antarctic continent to the South Pole. He arrived at the pole in January, 2003. At the time, he was 23 years, 268 days old.

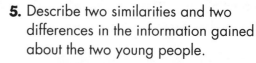

I won't skate around the issue. I'm the better skater.

1. Identify the tense of each verb in the sentences.

People celebrated Charlie Chaplin as one of the greatest actors of his time. Many movie buffs still love to watch his movies.

2. Insert commas where they belong.

Jonathan wanted to read biographies of astronauts drummers presidents firefighters and skateboarders.

3. What reference book is a geographical dictionary with places listed alphabetically?

○ a thesaurus

○ an almanac

○ a gazetteer

4. When Tara Lipinski won the Olympics, she had not yet turned professional in her sport. Was she a **novice** or an **amateur**?

5. Add a topic sentence.

Planet's Greatest Skateboarder

By age 16, he was well on his way to earning that reputation. Tony Hawk's fantastic skateboarding skill brought attention to the sport, and he is considered a pioneer of vertical skateboarding. He was the first skater in the world to land a 720-degree spin and a 900-degree spin. Retired from competition, Tony still has skateboard ramps in his yard, and floors adapted for skating in the house.

I'm a kick-flipper.

Read

1. What is the genre (kind) of writing?
2. What is the purpose of the selections?
3. What do Eileen Rollins and Lance Armstrong have in common?
4. How many hours has Eileen Collins spent in space?
5. Why was 2005 a good year for both of these people?

Eileen Collins has done something that no other woman has accomplished. In 2005, she became the first woman to pilot a space shuttle and the first to command a space shuttle mission. She headed up a team of astronauts who took a two-week mission on the space shuttle, *Discovery*. This was the first shuttle flight after the disastrous loss of the Columbia. A New York native, Eileen earned her pilot's license during college. Her pilot skills and good grades won her entry to the Air Force pilot training program. She became a flight instructor and aircraft commander for the Air Force. In 1990, NASA selected her to become an astronaut. She has flown in space four times, for a total of 872 space hours.

Lance Armstrong is known worldwide as the seven-time winner of the *Tour de France* bicycle race. That's seven times in a row from 1999 to 2005. No one else has accomplished this feat. He is also known as a cancer survivor. His dramatic recovery from cancer, combined with his determination to keep winning at his sport has earned him much admiration. A native of Texas, Lance was competing in triathlons by age 13 and riding in the Olympics at age 20. Besides cycling, he dedicates much energy to the Lance Armstrong Foundation to support cancer victims and survivors. Millions of people have bought yellow rubber "Livestrong" bracelets from the foundation to show their support for cancer awareness.

I knew that.

I did the research.

Write

Write the name of a person you know who fits each description. Then finish the sentence with a short explanation as to why you chose that person.

1. _____ is the most interesting person I know, because . . .
2. _____ is the most courageous person I know, because . . .
3. _____ is the person I would choose to be with me when I am very sad, because . . .
4. _____ is the person I would choose to be with me when I am in danger, because . . .
5. _____ is the funniest person I know, because . . .
6. _____ is the easiest person to be around, because . . .

1. Finish the analogy.

_____ : scalding :: cool : freezing

2. Circle letters that should be capitals.

The southernmost point in the united states of america is in the hawaiian islands, a place called ka lae.

3. Circle the predicate adjective(s).
Arizona is hot and dry.

4. To what sense does this passage have the strongest appeal?

Sweltering from the grueling sun and itchy from the evaporation of sweat all over her body, Suzie stopped to rest. "No, Suz, don't lean against the stabbing spires of that cactus!"

U.S. History
Look it up!

5. Number the lines to show the sequence in which these states gained statehood.

____ **New Mexico has been a state since 1912.**

____ **Alabama came into the Union 31 years after Massachusetts.**

____ **Pennsylvania became a state five days after Delaware.**

____ **Utah entered the Union in 1896.**

____ **Massachusetts became a state in July of 1788.**

____ **Kansas gained statehood in 1861.**

____ **Delaware was the first state.**

____ **Hawaii is the 50th state.**

1. The moniker of Michigan is "The Wolverine State." Find a synonym for **moniker**.

2. Correct any misspelled words.

A town in Lousiana has a speshul distinkshun. Rayne is the Frog Capitol of the World.

3. Rewrite the sentence with active verbs.
Frogs appear to be heading for town.

4. Write an introductory sentence or two for a speech that will entice people to visit Sheboygan, Wisconsin, the Bratwurst capital of the World, for a two-day Music and Bratwurst Festival

I'm in a state of confusion.

5. On which dictionary page would each of these words be found?

United States	underdog
unison	unfit

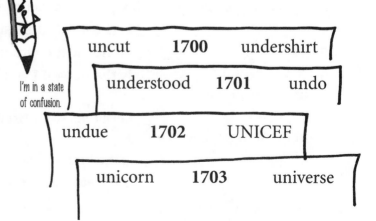

uncut	**1700**	undershirt
understood	**1701**	undo
undue	**1702**	UNICEF
unicorn	**1703**	universe

86

1. Choose the type of sentence.

○ interrogative   ○ imperative   ○ declarative

When you visit Lincoln, Nebraska, you must visit the Roller Skating Museum.

2. Circle the direct object. Draw a box around any indirect object.

Folks in Montana gave a glacier the name of Grasshopper Glacier because there were grasshoppers frozen in the ice.

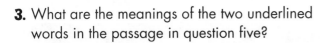

3. What are the meanings of the two underlined words in the passage in question five?

4. Write an alliterative sentence using some of these words.

Massachusetts	Mississippi
mustard	mysterious
monsters	mired

5. What causes the odious air in Kennet Square, Pennsylvania?

A moist, dark environment is needed for growing mushrooms. Furthermore, since mushrooms grow best on dead and decaying plant matter, plenty of fertilizer is also a requirement. That is why the little town of Kennet Square, Pennsylvania, is <u>infamous</u> for its <u>odious</u> air, as well as its successful mushroom crop. Visitors may hold their noses when they come to town, but the town's citizens are proud to produce 46 percent of the mushrooms in the U.S. and to call themselves the Mushroom Capital of the World.

We come from the Mushroom Capital of the World.

1. Add **ing** to each word.

explore	hurry	shovel	wish
plop	echo	suspect	vote

2. Write a homonym for eight words in the sentence.

This is a good week to visit the beaches of Florida. Shed your heavy clothes and idle away the days warming your pale skin in the sun or viewing the coral reefs.

3. Explain how nonfiction books are organized in a library.

4. Write a great title for the passage in example five.

Sock it to me.

5. Give the part of speech for each underlined word in the passage.

<u>Check</u> your socks! There is a <u>good</u> chance that <u>they</u> were made in Fort Payne, Alabama, the Sock Capital of the World. This area, the center of the U.S. hosiery <u>industry</u>, makes about 14 million pairs of socks a week. Right now, one in every seven Americans is wearing a pair of these socks. Are you? <u>Because</u> there is a threat from <u>Chinese</u> markets that can make lower-cost socks, locals <u>continually</u> hope that the U.S. government will limit sock <u>imports</u>.

Read

1. Draw the shape of your state (or province or country). Label it and the bordering states or areas.

2. Label major bodies of water and mountain ranges in or around it.

3. Draw the approximate location of any major Interstate highways that cross your state.

4. Draw a large star to locate the capital.

5. Draw a small star and label the location of your town or city.

6. Place symbols to show the major attractions or important features in the state.

My State _____

What is the state of your state?

State your reasons.

Key:

Oregon

I. **Size and Location**
   A. Pacific Northwest of U.S.
   B. Borders Pacific Ocean

II. **Geography**
   A. Land — mountains, valleys, desert in eastern part
   B. Water
      1. Borders Pacific Ocean
      2. Home to Crater Lake, deepest crater in U.S.
      3. Columbia River on northern border

III. **Special Features**
   A. Vast evergreen forests
   B. Rugged mountains
   C. Beautiful coastline

Write

Use the information from the outline in a paragraph description of some of Oregon's features.

1. Circle the prepositions in the sentences.

The Supreme Court is the highest court in the land. Justices serve for life.

2. Why are these words in the same group?

legality	failure	reversible
gladness	shrinkage	arguable

3. Fix the spelling errors.

A ladie in St. Louis seued a hair salan for a bad hair treetment. She won a six thousand doller settelment.

4. The conversation shows:

○ metaphor   ○ narration   ○ personification
○ stereotype   ○ irony   ○ foreshadowing

What is the difference between a lawyer and a herd of buffalo?

The lawyer charges more.

5. What questions should the defense lawyer (the attorney for the county) ask this woman about the incident?

A woman in West Palm Beach, Florida claimed that she suffered injuries because of a goose's behavior. Allegedly, the goose attacked her when she was trying to protect her child. She brought a lawsuit against the county, claiming that they were negligent in not protecting her from the goose.

I'm a watch-goose, so don't sue me.

1. What is the meaning of the underlined word?

Members of the jury were calmed and mesmerized by the <u>mellifluous</u> voice of the defense attorney.

2. Circle letters that should be capitals.

Two of the u. s. supreme court's most well-known decisions are miranda v. arizona and brown v. board of education.

I'm taking my case to the Supreme Court.

3. Circle the infinitive.

The Brown v. Board of Education decision made it illegal to segregate children of different races for educational purposes.

4. What is the purpose of an encyclopedia entry about the Supreme Court?

5. Write a short argument in favor of the suing passengers (the plaintiffs) or write a short argument against their claim for two million dollars.

A cross-continental flight ran into severe turbulence. For 28 seconds, some passengers not wearing their seatbelts were thrown from their seats. Some of the passengers sued, claiming the airline owed them money for the psychological distress of the moments of terror.

1. A jury found Sam Smurkel guilty of an unlawful deed. Was his behavior **elicit** or **illicit**?

2. Punctuate the sentence properly.

Ruth Bader Ginsberg the second woman to serve on the U.S. Supreme Court was appointed to her position in 1993

3. Rewrite the sentence to clarify the meaning.

The defendant brought a check to his lawyer wrapped in a brown envelope.

4. What is the main idea of the passage in question five?

5. What is the rhyme pattern of this poem?

Amanda ordered chowder.
She slurped it with delight.
Her husband saw the cockroach
But it slid down, out of sight.
She couldn't stop the swallow,
But she knew just what to do.
She grabbed the manager and choked,
"Ate a cockroach, I blame you.
In fact, what's more - I plan to sue."

Take your case to a higher court.

---

1. Circle the correct word.

My attorney gave good (advise, advice) when he told me not to pursue the lawsuit for bird droppings in my yard.

2. What is the denotation of **trial**?

3. Which examples show correct usage?

  a. Anyways, the case has gone to trial.

  b. That lawsuit was over real quick!

  c. The judge really was hard on the defendant.

  d. Surely, you aren't going to sue!

4. Give a title to the example in question five.

5. a. Which law is applicable to an entire state?

  b. Which law does not apply to humans?

Justice is blind.

Place	Prohibited Action
Baltimore, MD	taking a lion to a movie
Tennessee	lassoing a fish
Portland, OR	whistling underwater
Denver, CO	mistreating a rat
Virginia, MN	parking an elephant
Memphis, TN	frogs croaking past 11 p.m.

Read

1. Which client is asking for the largest settlement in court?

2. What do cases two and three have in common?

3. What is the meaning of the word **plaintiff** (case two)?

4. In which cases are the plaintiffs asking for money for pain or suffering?

5. Circle two puns in the selection.

Order in the court.

Here comes the judge.

Judge Les deBrief's Case Summaries

January 15

Case 1— Port v. Potato Chip Company

Mr. Port blames the Crunchy Potato Chip Company for his gain of 100 pounds. He claims that the potato chip bag label says the chips contain 200 calories. He understood that was the amount for the whole bag, and ate a bag every day for two years, believing it was a low-calorie snack. When he gained the weight, he became suspicious of the chips and had them analyzed. The chips contained 200 calories per serving, making a total of 2,000 calories in the bag. This information was not clear on the label. Mr. Port is suing for $3,000 to pay for a weight loss program.

Case 2 — Goat Owner v. O'Grady

The plaintiff, Belinda Bleet claims that her neighbor, Gus O'Grady is responsible for the death of her pet goat. She found the goat dead in her yard with smears of rancid chocolate pudding all over his face. Investigators found pools of the same substance in the Mr. O'Grady's garbage can. Belinda is asking for $10,000 for the goat's burial and to compensate for her pain and suffering at the loss of her beloved goat.

Case 3 — Neighbors v. Olive Family

Twelve neighbors from the 15th block of Neat Street are suing the Olive family for disturbing the neighborhood. They claim the visual disturbance is unacceptable. Two years ago, the Olives painted their home with wide, neon chartreuse stripes. They colored the grass on their lawn chartreuse, and even dyed the fur of their four dogs the same awful color. The neighbors claim this is offensive to their senses and lowers the property values. They are asking that the Olives be required by the court to remove the obnoxious color and to pay each neighbor $2,500 for the suffering they have occurred in looking at the sight. In his own defense, Mr. Olive accuses the neighbors of being green with envy over the beauty of his home.

Write

Write an outline of the judge's court cases for the day.
Include in the outline some of the major points about each case.

I wasn't sharp, so I'm in the slammer.

1. Find a pair of homonyms to fill in the blanks.

At ***Chocolates By Mueller*** in Philadelphia, a cardiologist needs _____ to wait in the long line to buy chocolate hearts for her favorite _____ (clients).

2. Does the pronoun agree with its antecedent?

A Malaysian restaurant in Boston has chicken feet on their menu.

3. The feeling in a piece of writing is the

○ theme ○ tone ○ mood
○ setting ○ point of view ○ plot

4. Fill in the blanks to show the tenses of the verb **eat**.

present: He is_____
past: She _____
future: He will_____

5. Follow the directions to draw a tasty strawberry, chocolate mousse parfait.

Draw these layers from the bottom up.

1. crushed Oreo cookies
2. chocolate mousse
3. sliced strawberries
4. chunky granola
5. chocolate mousse
6. whipped cream
7. whole strawberries
8. sprinkles of chocolate

Draw a spoon in the parfait.

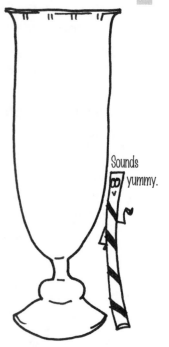

Sounds yummy.

1. Police took the cook at Bubba's Burgers to court for putting fingernail clippings into his burgers. Was the cook **persecuted** or **prosecuted**?

2. Insert commas correctly.

The cook at Bubba's by the way claimed that it was all a joke.

3. Circle the case of the pronoun.

subjective   objective

Mine is the one with the chocolate-covered onions.

4. What reference would you use to find the source of this famous quote?

An apple a day keeps the doctor away.

5. Rearrange the sentences for correct sequence.

It is an unusual food service, run by ninjas. The trouble is, everything is top secret, so no one knows who the customers are or whether the service actually exists. Supposedly, employees deliver fresh, hot food to special customers. The Ninja Burger Company was founded in 1954.

Eat at Ninjas

Ninja Burgers are tough!

1. Circle the correctly spelled words.

portsion   decision   locashun

invention   edision   reputasion

2. Write possessive phrases to show

a. the flavor of the sauce

b. the spices of many meatballs

c. the hats of several cooks

d. the choices on a menu

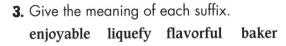

3. Give the meaning of each suffix.

enjoyable   liquefy   flavorful   baker

4. What literary technique is the comparison of two things that are not ordinarily alike?

○ metaphor   ○ hyperbole   ○ irony

○ imagery   ○ pun   ○ personification

5. Write a headline and a conclusion for the article.

_____

Last Saturday was not the best night for the elegant Chez Henri bistro. Customers did not want to be "chez" (with) Henri for long. Not far into the dinner hours, customers began shrieking, standing on their chairs, and running for the door. The cause of this distress was a horde of rats that found their way into the usually quiet, upscale restaurant.

---

1. The gourmand visited the Chez Henri bistro often. What is a **gourmand**?

2. Is a colon or semicolon needed? Add it to the sentence.

Customers don't mind waiting in line at Lynn's Paradise Café they can just climb a tree or play in the playhouse.

3. Circle the gerund phrase.

Eating at Lynn's Paradise Café is a unique and wonderful experience.

4. Choose the most precise word.

After the spicy sauce bit her tongue, she remarked, "My, this sauce is particularly _____."

○ tasty   ○ piquant   ○ acrid

5. Circle the restaurants whose names give you a clue to the kind of food they serve.

Restaurant Index

Beasey's Burgers, 6	Raja's Cuisine, 32
Chez Henri, 36	Ray's Hot Dogs, 34
The Dragonfly, 4	Sue's Subs, 30
Mama's Bakery, 19	Tasty Cone, 10
Mihama Grill, 16	Taste of Thai, 11
Natural Café, 9	Vinnie's, 28
O'Grady's, 15	Wayside Café, 23
Omar's, 22	White Pine Inn, 12
Pasta-A-Plenty, 17	Wraps & More, 25

Enjoy your meal.

Read

1. How many guests will Joe be serving?
2. What food precedes the pasta?
3. What is the meaning of **frutti de mare**?
4. What ingredients make up the salad?
5. What was the reason for Mario's mistake?

Joe Giacomini's Pasta Piatti

Menu
Governor's Dinner, March 10, 2006

Antipasto
Pate Dolce Vita

Zuppe
Minestrone Giacomini

Pasta
Linguini with Marinara Sauce, Basil Pesto, and
Sweet Sun-Dried Tomato Italian Sausage

Frutti de Mare
Shrimp Scampi a la Napoletana

Insalata Caprese
Fresh Slices Mozzarella, Tomatoes, and Basil

Dolce
Tiramisu

It was to be the biggest night of Joe's career as a top chef in this big city. Tonight, he would be serving all 50 state governors. His restaurant was chosen as the spot for their banquet solely because of Joe's reputation—especially the reputation for his famous linguini.

Everything was ready. The guests were already enjoying the pate. Joe's minestrone had never been so full of flavor, the tiramisu was perfect, and each insalata caprese was ready to be placed in front of a governor. The marinara sauce was simmering in a gigantic pot, its sweet basil aroma steaming up the kitchen. As Joe was busy testing and stirring the sauce, he directed his son, Mario, to drop the linguini noodles into the large pot of boiling water. Mario had just fallen in love that day, and was not paying attention as well as usual. Instead of 19 packages of noodles, Mario put 91 packages into the boiling water. That was the beginning of the greatest linguine disaster in the history of the city.

Write

Finish this cliffhanger. Tell what will happen next, and give the story a conclusion.

1. Choose the sentence type.

   ○ simple   ○ compound   ○ complex

   Soda pop machines are vending machines, and bubblegum machines operate in a similar way.

2. Circle words containing silent letters.

   Did you know that wooden tuning pins change the pitch of a piano's notes?

3. What is the meaning of this sentence?

   Don't lose your head just because you can't figure out how to work that 10-speed bicycle.

4. Choose the reporter's viewpoint

   ○ first person   ○ second person   ○ third person

   On a school field trip, Jed is watching the manufacture of a jet engine. As he watches, he talks into his voice recorder, describing everything he is seeing and thinking.

5. What allows a gumball to drop out of the container and roll out to you?

   At the base of the container, there is a metal plate with holes. Gumballs fall into those holes. When you put in a coin, the handle turns until a gumball lines up with an open slot. The gumball then falls through the slot and rolls down the runway—into your waiting hands.

Ka-ching!

1. Circle letters that should be capitals.

   toaster oven   norwegian cruise ship

   sears tower   american clock company

2. Count the adjectives.

   Each time you walk down a big city street, you're bound to see bright neon lights.

3. What is the meaning of **luminous**?

4. Which words would be found on a dictionary page with the guide words **neglectful** and **nerve**?

   ○ neon   ○ nervous

   ○ neither   ○ nerd

   ○ necessary   ○ nebula

5. Rewrite the passage for better sentence variety and flow.

   Neon lights are made from glass. The glass tubes are formed into particular shapes. The tubes are filled with neon gas. The tubes are sealed. An electrode (rod of solid iron) is sealed onto the ends of each tube. Electricity enters the electrodes. This makes some of the electrons jump around. Moving electrons cause bursts of light to light up the tube.

I work like clockwork.

1. Choose the antonyms for **conscientious**.
○ negligent   ○ heedless   ○ prudent   ○ careful

2. Circle the participial phrase.
The piece of bread burning in the toaster is my breakfast.

3. Correct the misspelled words.

abominable   reliable
invisibal   reversibal

Uh, oh!

4. Which examples contain a **simile**?
a. My toaster is a fiery dragon.
b. A toaster is like a bonfire.
c. Burned toast is brittle as glass.
d. Your hair is burned-toast black.

5. Write **F** (fact) or **O** (opinion) for each statement.

____ A toaster is more complicated to take apart than an alarm clock.

____ In most toasters, the toast pops up when it is done.

____ Unless it has a battery, an electric toaster needs to be plugged into a source of power.

____ All toasters will burn your toast in under two minutes.

____ Toasters last longer than alarm clocks.

1. Rewrite the sentence correctly
No garage door openers are sold there neither.

2. Write a word with a prefix meaning . . .
a. against germs
b. take wrong
c. operate together

3. Edit the passage.
When the light from a smoke detector bounces off smoke it reflects back to hit a photocell this sets off an alarm

4. Write a brief summary of the information given in question five.

Looks like I'm a little late.

5. What sets off the alarm?
How A Fire Sprinkler Works
• Heat from a fire warms the air.
• The warm air rises to the sprinkler head and breaks a seal on it.
• The force of water in the pipe pushes the cap off the sprinkler head.
• Water sprays from the sprinkler.
• Some water escapes through a side valve and spins a wheel, which sets off an alarm.

Name

Read

1. What is the main idea?
2. What is the genre (kind of writing)?
3. Is pencil lead made of lead?
4. Where does the eraser's raw material originate?

The story of my life is incredible. Do you get the point?

"The Pencil Story" is a fascinating opinion piece about what it takes to make a pencil. Its author is Nobel Prize winner and famous economist Milton Friedman. His opinion essay begins by saying, "Nobody knows how to make a pencil." As Friedman explains, the process of making a pencil actually takes hundreds of little steps that no single person can do. Someone makes the chainsaw and other equipment used to cut wood. It takes many people to manufacture, sell, and deliver this equipment. Others go into the forest to do the logging. Someone else buys, transports, and mills the wood. In another part of the world, usually South America, the material for the pencil lead (graphite) is mined from the ground. Someone makes, sells, and delivers the mining equipment. Others dig the graphite. Still others buy, sell, and ship it to the pencil companies. The material for the eraser is a substance that comes from another part of the world. Someone taps rubber trees in Malaysia. This goes through many stages of preparation, buying, selling, shipping, and delivering before it reaches the pencil manufacturer.

By the time all the supplies reach the place where the pencils are made, hundreds, perhaps thousands of people from all over the world have participated. The point of Friedman's writing is that no one person or company does this. People work together, without even knowing each other, to produce a product.

Write

Write a list of ten things for each of the lists.

Never clean your ears with a pencil. That would be bad.

10 Things Which Must Be Written With A Pencil

1.
2.
3.
4.
5.
6.
7.
8.
9.
10.

10 Things To Do With A Pencil

1.
2.
3.
4.
5.
6.
7.
8.
9.
10.

1. These are Joe's responses to the idea that his friend is a time traveler. Correct the spelling.

How peculier!   That's prepostrous!

It's scandilus.   I'm so jelous!

2. Fred and Ted had an **altercation** about the possibility of time travel. What does this mean?

3. Circle the letters of any true statements.

   a. A phrase has a subject and a predicate.

   b. An independent clause could stand alone as a complete sentence.

   c. A clause has a subject and a predicate.

   d. A dependent clause has no subject.

4. What is the bias of the person who wrote about the H.G. Wells book in question five?

5. What is the main idea of the passage?

In 1898, author H.G. Wells wrote a famous book about time travel: **The Time Machine**. In his story, a dreamer builds a time machine and tells some friends about this nutty idea of time travel. Then he climbs into the machine, or so he tells his friends later, and disappears. A week later, he arrives at dinner looking tired and tattered. The "time traveler" weaves a fantastic (and suspicious, I might add) tale about having traveled millions of years into the future. It's doubtful that anyone's friends would believe such a story!

The sands of Time are running.

1. Write a synonym for **reprehensible**.

2. Does the sentence show correct pronoun usage?

Lucy and I are very anxious to take a trip through a wormhole.

Watch it!

3. Add correct punctuation.

This is an interesting idea wormholes are tunnels through time and space

4. Which information can be found in a world almanac?

   a. a history of time travel

   b. record times for the latest Olympic races

   c. dates of major historical events

   d. information about recent scientific achievements

5. Rewrite the passage to include more interesting, colorful, active, or precise words or phrases. Pay special attention to replacing the underlined words.

Ask someone, "What is time?" They might <u>say</u>, "It is minutes and hours." This is a <u>hard</u> question, because we cannot <u>see</u> time. But the evidence of time is there. We can <u>see</u> our bodies <u>change</u>, the landscape <u>change</u>, and buildings <u>change</u>. We can define time in terms of changes, or in terms of <u>things</u> we can get done in a period of time.

1. Add correct punctuation and capitalization.

Are you sure asked jake that a black hole is a gateway to other universes

2. Finish the analogy.

_____ : inchworm :: timeline : overtime

3. Circle the interjection.

You have just returned from a trip into the future. How exciting!

4. Evaluate Charlie's reasoning.

"Time travel IS possible," insisted Charlie. "I know this because Einstein's theory claims that time slows as an object's speed gets closer to the speed of light. All you have to do is travel at the speed of light, and you'll catch up to the future."

5. Identify the literary technique used in each example.

a. Pete tells me he has traveled backward in time, but I don't believe him. I wasn't born yesterday!

b. Abigail's time machine eased through time like a bug crawling under a curtain.

c. "Here comes another time traveler," complained the wormhole to his neighbor.

The time is now!

1. Complete the sentence with one word that has two different meanings.

I'll _____ you with a gift that will help you travel backward from the _____.
(time being)

2. Name the underlined phrase.

That crazy professor <u>traveling in his time</u> machine is scaring the students.

I follow the sun.

3. Correct any misspelled words.

A time machine may be a conveneint way to fulfill your life-long dream of time travel. But beware, your nieghbors may shreik when you take off.

4. Explain the difference between a book's table of contents and its index.

5. Add at least two details about what happened on Sarah's trip.

The time machine was ready. So was Sarah. She said "Goodbye" to her friends, closed the door, and flipped the switch. ***Pffffft!*** The machine disappeared.

Just a few days later, looking rather ragged, Sara stepped out of the machine into her backyard. She was thrilled to have visited five past centuries.

Read

1. Which books are likely to be nonfiction?

2. Which book is the most expensive?

3. Which two books were written by the same author?

4. Which of the fiction books would come first on a library shelf?

There's nothing like a book.

The Bargain Bookstore

coupon book

all books on sale through the 31st

TIME MACHINES
K.S. THORNE
$49.95

THE ANCIENT ONE
T. A. Baron   *now* $13.95

SPACE TIME PHYSICS
Edwin F. Taylor
ONLY $55.95

𝒜 Wrinkle In Time
by
Madeline L'Engle
$12.95

𝒜 Wind In The Door
by
Madeline L'Engle
$10.95

Black Holes, Wormholes, & Time Machines
Jim Al-Khalili $25.95

How To Build A Time Machine
Paul Davies $14.95

Write

Assume that you are filling a time capsule with treasures and information from your life today. This will be buried, to be unearthed in 20 years. Complete these sentences for inclusion in the time capsule.

1. Presently, my life is _____

2. I value _____

3. Important people in my life are _____

4. My greatest joy is _____

5. I wish I could change _____

6. Something important to know about me is _____

7. The best memory in my life so far is _____

8. Ten years from now, I hope to be _____

Today's date is _____   My name is _____

1. What punctuation is missing?

Come along with us to Ojos del Salado that's the world's highest volcano; we're leaving tomorrow.

2. The most intense point of action in a story is its

○ resolution ○ theme ○ climax

○ theme ○ setting ○ plot

3. Is this the **connotation** or the **denotation** of breathtaking?

causing one to be out of breath; astonishing

4. Identify a cause and an effect.

About three miles below Niagara Falls is a deep, round basin that has been carved out by the violent currents from the steep falls.

5. Identify each sentence as **D** (declarative), **IN** (interrogative), **IM** (imperative), or **E** (exclamatory)

____ a. Get a picture of this statue of Crazy Horse.

____ b. Let's travel the entire length of the Great Wall of China.

____ c. Have you seen Niagara Falls?

____ d. No, we went to the Taj Mahal.

____ e. Don't drop the camera.

____ f. Watch out for falling rocks!

I took great photos of the Great Wall and the Taj Mahal.

1. Correct the misspelled words.

Let's visit the Grand Canion and ride donkies all the way to the bottem.

2. What is the meaning of the root that these words have in common?

portable	**transport**	**porter**
deported	**portage**	**import**

3. Correct the usage errors.

Bob and Lou they shouldn't have never tried to climb up to Machu Picchu alone.

4. What reference book is a collection of articles telling about the lives of people and their accomplishments, arranged alphabetically?

5. Classify the pronouns.

interrogative _____

possessive _____

singular _____

demonstrative _____

plural _____

indefinite _____

ours	**that**	**whatever**
both	**it**	**some**
hers	**which**	**somebody**

I've always wanted to see the queen's throne.

1. Why are quotation marks used in this sentence?

The Great Wall of China gives a whole new meaning to the word "long."

2. Circle the appositive.

Machu Picchu, Peru's main tourist attraction, is a site of ancient ruins built high in the Andes Mountains.

3. Find a pair of homonyms to complete each sentence.

a. Our ship is headed _____ through the _____ of Gibraltar.

b. The _____ of both yachts wanted to _____ past the Statue of Liberty.
     (sail)

4. Which stickers in question five are similes?

5. What can you infer about the owner of this suitcase?

Gateway Arch
As high as the heavens

Look the Great Sphinx in the eye!

Sharp like a dagger
THE SPACE NEEDLE

The bells are ringing!
London Tower

Amazing Ruins!
Chichen Itza

Cruise Through It
Panama Canal

1. Why are these classified together?

daring   audacious   valiant   intrepid

2. Correct this sentence.

You'll need to choose among these two: see the Roman Ruins or New York City.

3. Correct any spelling errors

The Parthenon was dameged in 1687 when the Venetians tried to concquer Athens. Only rooins remain.

I make a point of visiting the wonders of the world

4. An encyclopedia entry for Machu Picchu would be found on a page with the guidewords

a. Picasso and Pike's Peak

b. mackerel and Madeira Islands

c. Macedonia and McKinley

5. Rewrite this poem as prose.

China built an awesome wall
Four thousand miles and that's not all.
Begun by ancient dynasties
To keep out fearsome enemies,
It stretches far across the land,
All pieces put in place by hand.
It loops and twists o'er rocks and rills.
It crosses deserts, vales, and hills.
With years, decay and ruin came,
But now they say that it's a shame.
And so, they'll try to fix the wall.
And that's good news for one and all.

Name

Index *(for a book on World Wonders)*

Angel Falls, 86
bridge, 23
canal, 37
canyon, 28
caves, 78
Chichen Itza, 90
Christ the Redeemer Statue, 55
Eiffel Tower, 7
falls, 15, 86
Gateway Arch, 19
glacier, 83
Great Sphinx, 53

Great Wall of China, 61
Grand Canyon, 28
Lambert-Fischer Glacier, 83
Leaning Tower of Pisa, 48
London Bridge, 23
Machu Picchu, 46
Mammoth Cave, 78
Mona Lisa, 12
Mt. Rushmore, 41
Niagara Falls, 15
Notre Dame, 9
paintings, 12

Panama Canal, 37
Parthenon, 69
Pyramids, 58
ruins, 46, 75, 90
Space Needle, 26
statues, 41, 53, 55, 72, 75
Statue of Liberty, 72
Stonehenge, 75
Sydney Opera House, 65
Taj Mahal, 84
Tower of London, 35
towers, 7, 35, 48

What a list!

Read

1. How many different statues are listed in the index?

2. How long is the section on the Parthenon?

3. Name three natural wonders covered in this book.

4. On what pages will you find information on the Taj Mahal?

Write

Write two postcards from one of the wonderful world places in the index above. Write each one to a different audience—for instance, to a young child, to a good friend who is your own age, to a parent, to a grandparent, or to a teacher.

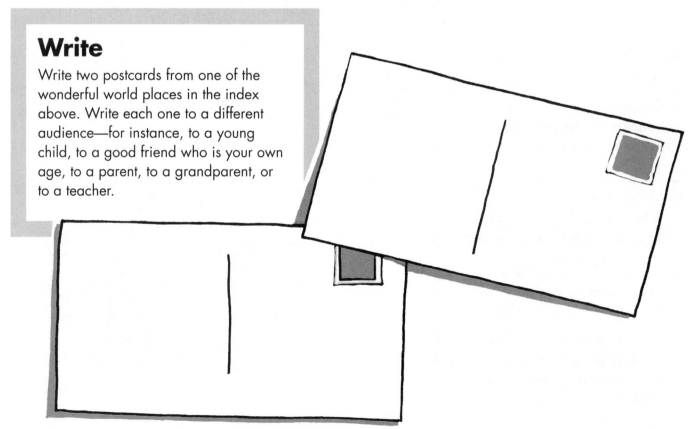

Use It! Don't Lose It! IP 612-2

1. What elements should be included before the greeting of a business letter?

2. Tell the part of speech of each underlined word in the sentence.

   <u>Every</u> year, the Disneyland lost-and-found department <u>faithfully</u> collects thousands of lost <u>objects</u>.

3. What is a **marauder**?

4. Choose the literary technique used in this opening sentence from a student's story.

   My dog gets lost at least a thousand times a week.

   ○ hyperbole   ○ personification

   ○ onomatopoeia   ○ satire

   ○ alliteration   ○ foreshadowing

5. What objects are most commonly lost at Disneyland?

   A surprising number of objects are lost at Disneyland—as many as 140,000 objects a year. Most of these are sunglasses and hats, but many are jewelry, cell phones, and palm pilots. The woman who ran the lost-and-found department for 20 years took delight in returning such things as lost engagement rings, cameras, or toupees to their owners. Once, when she found a name and number on an expensive camera, she contacted the family. The family had not been to Disneyland, but the burglar who stole the camera from their home had been!

1. Find a synonym for **incorrigible**.

2. Choose the correct word.

   The Crocker family stayed in the (desert, dessert) for three weeks.

3. Circle any linking verbs. Draw a box around action verbs.

   It is a miracle that Chester (our hamster) found his way home.

4. Choose the most precise word to complete the sentence.

   ○ odd   ○ garish

   ○ displeasing   ○ unattractive

   Sue was not sorry that her sister lost that chartreuse, rhinestone-covered jacket with a feather collar. It was so_____ anyway.

5. Which personal item was never found?

Personal Lost & Found

Date Lost	Lost Item	Time Lost	Found?
1-3-03	gerbil	18 days	yes
1-30-03	ski hat	3 years	no
7-12-03	sister	1 hour	yes
10-23-04	book report	3 days	yes
3-10-05	baseball glove	9 weeks	yes
12-20-05	mom's diamond	2 days	yes

1. What word could be added to each of these to make a compound word?

size   touch   break   stairs   town

2. Add **-ing** and **-ed** to each word.

search   marry   echo   stub   match

3. Which examples show correct usage?

a. Is it Sam for whom you are searching?

b. Who's parrot is lost?

c. Whomever is lost, we'll find her.

d. Grandma's the one whose lost.

4. Choose the literary device used in the sentence.

○ imagery   ○ metaphor
○ simile   ○ hyperbole
○ alliteration ○ pun

Lost in the world, she's a soft clam without a shell.

5. Circle the cause in each example.

a. A whale swam into the river in London, alarming the citizens.

b. The whale is confused, so it is swimming upstream.

Circle the effect in each example.

c. When whales turn up in strange places, it is usually because they are sick or wounded.

d. Officials ran into the water to push the whale back to deeper water when it got stuck.

Being lost makes me wail.

1. Which words need capital letters?

ellen mcfaul was the manager of disneyland's lost-and-found department for 20 years.

2. Circle antonyms for **bewilder**.

baffle   enlighten   clarify   confuse   explain

3. Edit this sentence.

in january of 2006 a lost whale swam up the river thames in central london

4. Correct the usage.

The searchers did good to find the girl whom has been lost for a week.

5. Number these movie titles in alphabetical order.

___ *Lost in Chicago*

___ *Lost and Found Before Dinner*

___ *Lost: A Talking Python*

___ *The Last Rescue Party*

___ *Looking for the Lost Swimmer*

___ *Locating Laramie*

___ *Lost on the Way to the Outhouse*

I lost my cool.

We didn't make the list this time.

SCAVENGER HUNT LIST

Find each one.
Bring back a sample or a picture.

lozenge	sieve
portrait	cul-de-sac
veranda	lariat
artichoke	moccasin
sonata	lien
tycoon	parfait
debris	thyme
brooch	bridle
query	belt buckle

Find something that is . . .
(Bring back a sample or a picture.)

taffeta	braised
miniscule	congealed
fexible	euphonic
caustic	impenetrable
legible	crimson

Read

Read this list that has been prepared for a scavenger hunt.

1. For each item in the top section, tell where you would look. You may need a dictionary to sort out the meanings of the words.

2. For each adjective in the bottom section, name an item you might find that would match the description.

LOST

100 cans of sauerkraut

FOUND

an inner tube filled with Jello

LOST

a pet skunk

Write

Create a classified ad for each of the lost or found items.

1. Give correct capitalization to the CD cover.

2. Circle the complete predicate.
The Beatles have sold more than a billion discs and tapes.

TUNES
TO
MATCH YOUR
HULA-HOOPING

3. What is the meaning of the underlined word?
After the party, all my CDs were missing. Someone must have <u>absconded</u> with them.

4. The sentence below is an example of
○ personification   ○ simile
○ hyperbole   ○ metaphor
That new CD by the String Cheese Band called my name from the rack in the music store.

Wheeeee!

5. Number the sentences in a sensible sequence.

____ They got the reward for their hard work when they were invited to play for some school dances.

____ Before long, their music started sounding very good.

____ Michael, Keesha, and Danny met in junior high.

____ They began to practice in Danny's garage every day after school.

____ This is when they discovered their mutual dream of starting a band.

____ Friends started coming around and listening.

1. Correct the usage errors.
a. **How come you like hip-hop music?**
b. **Where is the drummer at?**

2. Circle the correctly spelled words.
simeltaneously   percipitation
hippopotomus   perpendicaler
biodegradable   brontosaurus

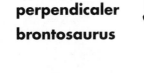

3. Finish the analogy.
electricity : electrician :: _____ : drummer

4. Which key word is best for an encyclopedia search on the Grammy Awards?
○ ceremony   ○ awards
○ Grammy   ○ music

5. Rewrite the sentences to make them more interesting and the verbs active.

a. **Jojo is drumming wildly.**

b. **The music coming out of the garage seems to be awfully loud.**

c. **Arianna's voice is so strong that her singing sounds powerful.**

d. **The drummer's hair appears to sway as she plays the drums.**

1. Several fans at a recent concert openly broke the rules for acceptable conduct. Did they **flout** or **flaunt** the rules?

2. Insert apostrophes correctly.

Isnt it interesting that the bands original name was the Blue Cheese String Band?

3. Details in a piece of literature that appeal to the senses are examples of

○ tone   ○ themes   ○ imagery

○ similes   ○ metaphors   ○ rhymes

4. Circle and identify the verbal in each sentence (gerund, infinitive, participle).

a. The screeching hurts my ears.

b. Drumming is Michael's gift.

c. Fans spinning hoops stayed late.

d. They were reluctant to stop dancing.

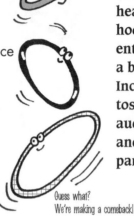

Guess what?
We're making a comeback!

5. What is the main idea of the passage?

Hula hooping is not just for kids anymore. In fact, hula hooping is not even called that anymore. The "hula" has been dropped. Now, it's just "hooping," and it has caught on with adults. "Hoopers," as they call themselves, spin hoops that are heavier and larger than the old plastic hoops of the 1950s. The revival of enthusiasm for hooping is credited to a band called The String Cheese Incident. At their concerts, they tossed hoops into the crowd to get the audience dancing. The idea caught on and spread to concerts, dances, and parties around the country.

1. Some of the band's fans were **obstreperous**. What does this mean?

2. Circle the direct object(s).

Brooks and Dunn have recorded 17 number one hits.

3. What category of writing could this be?

○ fiction   ○ nonfiction   ○ biography

Members of the band Dewey Decimal and the System have written a story about some of their experiences on the road.

4. Correct the spelling.

gutair	**popularaty**
qouartet	**audatorium**
microphone	**managment**

5. Write a caption for the picture.

Name

CD insert

Read

1. Who is the publisher for the band's new album?
2. Which hit single would you most like to hear?
3. Which member of the band has a country music background?
4. Which band member plays an electronic instrument?

CD cover

Write

Write eight words or descriptive phrases for each band member. Include words that pertain to their looks, movements, and personalities.

Dewey	Zed	B.B.	Kelly	Veronica

1. For each example, tell if the verb is an action verb or a linking verb.

   a. The story of Atlantis is a great legend.

   b. An earthquake destroyed the island

   c. An entire continent slipped into the sea.

   d. The legend appears to have little truth.

2. Circle each correctly spelled word.

   business   **busyness**   **busness**

   restrant   **restarant**   **restaurant**

   nuisence   **nusance**   **nuisance**

3. Write a synonym for **fantasy**.

4. What literary technique is extreme exaggeration used to increase the effects of a statement or story?

5. Make an inference about what you might see or learn in each movie.

Poseidon, the Great Sea God

How To Recover Sunken Treasure

Mermaids: Fact or Fiction

The Lost City of Atlantis

A City Under Water

I wish I had a T.V.

1. Some think that the whole idea of the island culture in Atlantis is **farcical**. What does this mean?

2. Does the sentence show correct use of a dash?

   That earthquake—the one that sank Atlantis, destroyed an entire culture.

3. Rewrite this to clarify the meaning.

   Mermaids caught the attention of sailors combing their hair and singing while sitting on the rocks.

4. Think of five words that could be found on a glossary page with the guidewords **Antarctica** and **Atlantis**.

I think I see a mermaid.

5. Edit the questions.

   • Is their eny truth to the storys about mermaids

   • I hear that tales of mermaids are unaversal; who was frist to tell them?

   • Are mermaids alwis female? Arent their any mails?

   • Has anywon seen the skulpture of the mermaid in Copenhagen harbur?

   • Is it true that mermaids washt up in Malasia after the 2004 sunamie?

1. What is the meaning of the sentence?

Will is burning the candle at both ends with his nonstop reading about Atlantis.

2. Circle the silent letters.

schedule **chorus** **budge**

wrestler **gnash** **pseudonym**

3. Does the subject agree with the verb?

Groups of sailors claim to have seen mermaids on the rocks.

4. Tell if each statement is true or false.

____ a. Narrative writing tells a story about events that have happened.

____ b. Narrative writing can be about real or imaginary events.

5. Why might manatees be the explanation behind the mermaid stories?

The manatee is a sea creature that might have been unfamiliar to sailors in the era of the first mermaid stories. Manatees cradle their young in their arms, much as a woman would carry a baby. The manatees have a strong tail. Often they rise to the surface through seaweed, with the seaweed streaming over their heads. These creatures basked on rocks in the sun.

The first-known mermaid stories were told about 1000 BC in Assyria. Sailors spoke of beings with the heads and torsos of human females, long hair, and fish tails. They said that the creatures came up out of the sea with their long hair streaming down their bodies and basked on rocks.

I am beautiful.

1. Give the meaning of each root.

marina **geology**

durable **cryptic**

2. Edit the sentence.

mermaids legendary aquatic creatures seem to be part fish and part human

3. Publications such as newspapers, journals, and magazines that are issued at regular intervals are

○ thesauruses ○ periodicals ○ atlases

4. What kind of phrase is italicized?

Mermaids are some *of the most famous creatures* in literature.

Peek-a-boo!

5. Eliminate unnecessary words.

The movie, ***Splash***, is a movie that tells the story of a mermaid who fell in love with a human man. When she is on dry land and not in the sea, the mermaid looks normal. When any water is splashed on her legs, her legs they change into a fishtail that looks like the tail of a fish. The central main theme of the movie revolves around her efforts to keep her boyfriend from learning or finding out that she is a mermaid.

Name

Write

1. Edit the passage to improve the flow of the sentences and to correct the grammar and spelling.

2. Give the passage a good title.

For centuries, people have been fascinated with platos tales about the legendary contenent of atlantis. Plato a writer in ancient grease wove a tale of a great empire that existed on an island continent. According to him this was a brillyant civilisation with magnificent citys and riches. The kingdom, it was created and ruled by Poseidon the god of the see.

After many years of prosperus life under poseidons laws trouble brewed in atlantis. Its people became proud and greedy, and forgot the laws that kept the civilization running smoothly So, the story goes, the gods they punished Atlantis. A great earthquake shook the whole contenent, bringing on floods and storms the whole island sank into the sea.

This story incites the imagination many wonders if Atlantis was real or just another greak Myth. There are those who believe it did exist and some who think the story doesn't have no basis in fact. Some think the great City still lies beneath the Ocean inhabited by see creatures such as mermades and mermen. Many expedations have tried to discover the remains of the island. There are even some predictions that the contenent will again raise from the sea.

Could a real place have inspired platos imagination. Some scientists and scholars think so. The aegean island of Thira was distroyed in 1470 B.C by a valcanic eruption this desaster wiped out a large portion of the Minoan civilization.

Read

1. What is the meaning of **incite** in the third paragraph?

2. Who supposedly founded the civilization of Atlantis?

3. According to Plato's story, what caused the end of Atlantis?

4. What do you wish to be true about this story?

INCENTIVE PUBLICATIONS DAILY PRACTICE SERIES
GRADE 7 LANGUAGE SKILLS

Vocabulary & Word Skills

Skill	1	2	3	4	5	6	7	8	9	10	11	12	13	14	15	16	17	18	19	20	21	22	23	24	25	26	27	28	29	30	31	32	33	34	35	36
Prefix, suffix, and root meanings	√		√			√			√			√			√			√			√					√		√		√	√					√
Compound words		√			√			√			√						√						√				√							√	√	
Knowledge of word meanings	√			√		√	√		√		√		√			√		√			√					√		√		√	√	√		√		√
Word and phrase meaning from context	√			√					√				√				√	√		√			√	√			√		√							√
Denotation and connotation		√						√							√			√			√								√							
Identify synonyms	√				√					√	√		√			√						√		√				√		√		√		√		√
Identify antonyms		√			√			√		√	√		√			√	√			√		√				√			√		√			√		
Words with similar meanings or sounds						√			√					√	√	√		√		√		√			√		√		√			√				
Homonyms		√	√	√			√			√				√		√			√				√			√		√				√			√	
Multiple meanings					√						√								√	√	√			√		√	√					√	√			√
Meanings of figurative language		√	√				√	√			√		√		√	√	√		√	√	√				√			√	√							
Word classification		√	√								√										√															
Analogies			√	√			√			√			√	√	√	√	√	√	√			√		√			√	√		√		√			√	

Reading Comprehension

Skill	1	2	3	4	5	6	7	8	9	10	11	12	13	14	15	16	17	18	19	20	21	22	23	24	25	26	27	28	29	30	31	32	33	34	35	36
Main ideas	√	√	√	√	√			√			√		√		√				√			√			√	√	√	√	√	√	√	√		√	√	√
Supporting details	√	√	√	√	√	√	√	√	√	√	√		√	√	√	√	√	√	√	√	√	√	√	√	√		√	√	√	√	√		√	√		√
Sequence	√	√			√				√				√			√		√			√		√	√			√	√		√						√
Read titles, headlines, captions					√	√				√			√		√			√		√	√						√			√						√
Follow directions				√		√			√										√	√					√											
Find information	√	√	√	√	√	√	√	√	√	√	√	√	√	√			×		√	√	√	√	√	√	√	√	√	√	√	√			√		√	√
Fact and opinion	√	√			√							√					√				√							√			√					
Cause and effect		√		√		√									√									√			√		√							
Interpret graphs, tables, illustrations, graphics		√		√						√	√		√			√	√					√	√		√		√			√			√	√		
Draw conclusions	√	√						√		√	√				√	√		√	√	√	√			√		√		√	√	√	√	√				√
Make inferences	√	√	√						√					√				√				√							√	√		√	√	√		√
Make predictions					√												√			√					√			√			√					
Compare and contrast	√		√					√					√	√	√	√						√		√		√	√		√	√		√		√		√
Summarize			√	√		√	√	√	√						√					√						√		√	√	√		√				
Evaluate		√			√		√	√		√			√					√		√		√		√			√	√	√		√	√				

113

©2006 Incentive Publications, Inc., Nashville, TN

INCENTIVE PUBLICATIONS DAILY PRACTICE SERIES
GRADE 7 LANGUAGE SKILLS

Literature

Skill	1	2	3	4	5	6	7	8	9	10	11	12	13	14	15	16	17	18	19	20	21	22	23	24	25	26	27	28	29	30	31	32	33	34	35	36
Identify setting, plot, characters, theme, tone, mood, point of view	√																																			
Identify writing genres and modes			√		√		√	√	√		√	√	√	√	√	√		√	√	√	√	√	√	√	√	√	√	√	√	√	√		√		√	√
Identify literary devices: simile, metaphor, alliteration, puns, rhyme, rhythm, repetition, personification, imagery, hyperbole, onomatopoeia, idioms, foreshadowing	√			√		√		√	√	√	√	√	√	√	√	√	√	√	√	√	√	√	√	√	√		√	√	√	√			√	√		√
Identify stereotypes and bias		√									√	√									√	√	√						√	√						
Identify author's audience and purpose					√	√			√	√	√		√	√			√				√		√	√			√						√			
Identify rhyming patterns of poems	√																√				√							√	√							
Identify writing techniques	√		√		√	√			√	√	√		√	√	√		√	√	√	√	√	√	√	√	√			√					√		√	√

Writing

Skill	1	2	3	4	5	6	7	8	9	10	11	12	13	14	15	16	17	18	19	20	21	22	23	24	25	26	27	28	29	30	31	32	33	34	35	36
Choose effective words	√		√		√	√	√										√	√			√	√	√	√			√	√	√	√		√		√	√	
Eliminate repetitive or unnecessary words or phrases			√							√	√	√	√		√				√	√	√	√		√		√	√		√		√					√
Write in different genres and modes	√	√	√				√	√	√	√	√	√	√	√	√			√	√	√	√	√	√	√		√	√	√	√	√	√		√		√	
Write prose and poetry	√	√	√			√	√	√	√	√	√	√		√	√			√	√	√	√	√	√			√	√	√	√	√		√	√		√	
Write topic sentences	√					√		√				√											√		√		√	√								
Add supporting details			√	√		√				√	√				√			√		√	√				√					√		√				
Write strong beginnings, endings							√																						√							
Write effective titles, captions, headlines	√	√	√					√		√					√	√			√		√	√		√	√	√	√	√		√			√			√
Summarize a written piece	√	√							√		√		√	√	√		√				√	√	√	√	√	√	√		√	√	√	√	√	√	√	√
Respond to a written piece	√		√		√		√		√	√									√		√	√	√	√	√	√	√	√	√	√		√				√
Revise for clarity, word choice, effectiveness, sequence, flow	√				√		√			√		√	√			√	√			√		√	√	√	√	√	√	√	√		√	√	√	√	√	√
Edit sentences for spelling, usage, punctuation, and capitalization		√	√						√			√									√		√	√	√			√			√			√		√

114

©2006 Incentive Publications, Inc., Nashville, TN

INCENTIVE PUBLICATIONS DAILY PRACTICE SERIES GRADE 7 LANGUAGE SKILLS

Grammar

Skill	1	2	3	4	5	6	7	8	9	10	11	12	13	14	15	16	17	18	19	20	21	22	23	24	25	26	27	28	29	30	31	32	33	34	35	36
Sentences (completeness, kinds: complexity, purpose)	✓	✓																		✓							✓	✓			✓					
Subjects and predicates	✓			✓											✓													✓					✓		✓	
Predicate nouns and adjectives								✓		✓										✓	✓			✓		✓		✓								
Conjunctions and interjections				✓															✓												✓					
Parts of speech	✓	✓		✓		✓	✓	✓	✓	✓	✓		✓		✓		✓	✓	✓	✓	✓		✓					✓			✓	✓		✓		
Common, proper nouns		✓				✓		✓						✓			✓			✓		✓		✓				✓			✓	✓				
Singular, plural nouns			✓	✓										✓				✓		✓				✓												✓
Possessive nouns			✓			✓				✓				✓	✓		✓					✓		✓			✓								✓	
Kinds of pronouns		✓		✓				✓								✓	✓			✓			✓										✓			
Verb tenses (regular, irregular)			✓	✓	✓		✓		✓					✓		✓	✓		✓			✓				✓								✓		
Case: nominative, objective				✓															✓											✓						
Action and linking verbs						✓							✓		✓	✓										✓								✓		
Transitive and intransitive verbs																																				
Verbals (participles, infinitives, gerunds)											✓												✓						✓	✓	✓	✓			✓	
Comparative and superlative adjectives, adverbs					✓										✓					✓	✓									✓					✓	
Direct and indirect objects						✓				✓								✓		✓		✓						✓								
Prepositions						✓					✓		✓					✓				✓							✓		✓	✓			✓	
Phrases							✓	✓			✓			✓	✓								✓		✓				✓		✓	✓	✓			✓
Appositives							✓	✓											✓														✓		✓	
Misplaced modifiers												✓					✓			✓		✓					✓						✓		✓	
Clause; distinguish between clauses and phrases														✓								✓										✓				

Use It! Don't Lose It! IP 612-2

Usage

Skill	1	2	3	4	5	6	7	8	9	10	11	12	13	14	15	16	17	18	19	20	21	22	23	24	25	26	27	28	29	30	31	32	33	34	35	36
Subject-verb agreement			√		√					√		√	√			√	√										√									√
Pronoun-antecedent agreement							√									√			√											√			√			
Use of *who, whom, whoever,* and *whomever*	√				√				√									√				√														
Use of *who's* and *whose*											√															√										
Subject and object pronoun use		√		√					√			√								√					√							√				
Use of negatives	√					√		√					√																		√	√				
Usage of adjectives-adverbs that are easily confused			√						√						√							√	√						√				√	√		
Other usage errors			√					√	√					√									√	√					√						√	√

Capitalization & Punctuation

Skill	1	2	3	4	5	6	7	8	9	10	11	12	13	14	15	16	17	18	19	20	21	22	23	24	25	26	27	28	29	30	31	32	33	34	35	36
Capitalization of proper nouns and adjectives	√	√		√	√	√	√	√	√	√	√	√	√	√	√	√	√	√		√		√	√	√	√	√	√	√	√	√	√	√	√	√		√
Capitalization in titles							√	√			√							√					√	√				√	√							
Commas		√		√	√		√	√	√	√	√	√	√	√	√	√			√	√	√	√	√	√	√		√	√	√	√	√	√	√	√		√
Ending punctuation	√	√		√	√	√	√		√	√	√	√	√	√	√			√		√		√	√					√	√		√	√		√		√
Colons, semicolons			√			√		√	√										√						√							√				√
Quotation marks				√		√	√			√			√						√	√			√			√	√					√	√			
Hyphens, dashes, parentheses, and ellipses					√									√	√							√	√				√			√						√
Apostrophes	√	√	√	√	√	√	√	√	√	√	√	√	√	√		√	√	√	√	√	√	√	√	√	√	√	√	√	√		√	√	√	√	√	√
Capitalization and punctuation in sentences and titles			√	√							√			√	√				√		√			√		√				√			√		√	√
Capitalization and punctuation in quotations						√				√								√				√		√		√						√		√		
Capitalization and punctuation in letters					√										√							√	√											√	√	

©2006 Incentive Publications, Inc., Nashville, TN

Use It! Don't Lose It! IP 612-2

INCENTIVE PUBLICATIONS DAILY PRACTICE SERIES
GRADE 7 LANGUAGE SKILLS

Spelling

Skill	1	2	3	4	5	6	7	8	9	10	11	12	13	14	15	16	17	18	19	20	21	22	23	24	25	26	27	28	29	30	31	32	33	34	35	36
Words with ie	√												√						√													√				
Confusing consonant and vowel spellings							√			√																						√			√	√
Singular and plural nouns			√	√				√				√					√	√		√	√			√											√	√
Past tense of verbs				√	√							√		√				√				√		√	√									√		
Words with silent letters						√						√						√					√		√				√		√					√
Words with final y									√							√				√				√				√					√			√
Words that end in o				√				√				√				√																				
Correct spelling of endings					√	√					√	√	√		√			√					√	√		√		√		√		√	√		√	√
Confusing words					√						√															√										
Identify correctly spelled words	√	√				√				√	√		√		√						√							√	√	√		√	√	√		
Correct misspelled words		√	√	√			√	√	√		√		√	√		√				√		√	√	√			√	√	√	√	√		√	√	√	√
Spell words correctly		√	√	√	√	√	√	√	√		√	√	√	√		√	√	√		√	√		√	√	√		√		√	√	√		√		√	√

Study & Research Skills

Skill	1	2	3	4	5	6	7	8	9	10	11	12	13	14	15	16	17	18	19	20	21	22	23	24	25	26	27	28	29	30	31	32	33	34	35	36
Alphabetical order	√			√									√						√															√		
Guide words			√			√								√			√		√			√						√			√					√
Key words			√														√									√									√	
Dictionary, encyclopedia entries					√						√						√						√					√	√				√			
Purposes and uses of different reference materials			√					√				√						√				√								√						√
Parts of a book	√					√																			√							√				
Information from a map, illustration, diagram, other graphics	√	√		√			√			√									√					√					√				√			
Information from tables, charts, timelines, outlines, indexes					√		√				√					√		√		√	√		√			√		√	√					√		
Fiction, biography, non-fiction				√												√					√			√			√	√				√	√			
Library organization				√					√									√			√			√							√	√				

Use It! Don't Lose It! IP 612-2

ANSWER KEY

Week 1 (pages 5–7)

MONDAY
1. Legends, Kraken, Marie, Celeste, Scandinavian
2. im, in, non, un, il
3. Answers will vary. One possibility: The Kraken has long, slimy tentacles.
4. poetry
5. b, c

TUESDAY
1. period
2. a table of contents
3. Mythical creatures, such as mermaids and mermen,
4. yes
5. Answers may vary somewhat. Cross out it is thought that, made up of two different animals, sailing by, so the stories say, the distractions

WEDNESDAY
1. a-b-b-b
2. piece, weigh, either
3. ridiculed, made fun of
4. a, c
5. By 2001, he had gathered over 4,000 reports of incidents involving some large creature.

THURSDAY
1. noun
2. startled
3. 1 beggar; 2 biennial; 3 bifocal; 4 Bigfoot; 5 bighearted; 6 bijou
4. dubious, doubtful, suspicious
5. John Green, a newspaper reporter from British Columbia, followed stories of the Sasquatch for almost 50 years. He believes that the existence of the Sasquatch has never been proved. However, he points out two things that have been proved: the existence of some huge deep footprints, and the thousands of credible people who claim to have seen a large, hairy, bipedal creature.

FRIDAY
Read:
1. There is a legend about a monster living in Scotland's Loch Ness. Some believe in the Loch Ness Monster; others do not.
2. sense of sight
3. Thousands seek to see her. Thousands more will try. AND the last two lines
4. monster, legend, creature, serpent
5. Drawings will vary.
Write: Summaries and titles will vary. Some people believe that a large monster with a long neck and broad head lives in Loch Ness, Scotland. Many are attracted to search for the monster, but there is no certainty that she is there. A video supposedly captures a picture of the monster, but its authenticity is in question. The poet believes Nessie exists, and is setting off to search for her.

Week 2 (pages 8–10)

MONDAY
1. Titanic, St. John's Glacier, Bering Sea
2. For most icebergs, such as the one that was hit by the Titanic, nine-tenths of the mass is below the surface of the water.
3. icicle, defrost, sinkable, submerge
4. no
5. Answers many vary: wants visitors to have fun, appreciates glaciers

TUESDAY
1. b
2. criticize, televise
3. Answers will vary: they, them, their, theirs, themselves, her, hers, she, him, he, his, himself, herself
4. 519
5. a, c, e

WEDNESDAY
1. b
2. candor
3. The Day the Titanic Sank (alternative The Day The Titanic Sank)
4. Cause: Snow falls and stays on the ground all year long. Eventually it packs down, hardens, Effect: and forms glaciers
5. to inform

THURSDAY
1. Answers will vary: a sea animal, a sticky piece that holds something shut, to fasten something shut, to confirm something
2. many, weather (or whether), amuse, empty, history, caught
3. b, d
4. Topic sentences will vary.
5. Predictions will vary.

FRIDAY
Read:
1. the load of rocks, boulders, and debris that the glacier carries along as it moves
2. Ice from the glacier melts and collects in cirques.
3. the water resulting from melting ice
4. It is logical to conclude that the abrading is done by the till.
5. Outwash is debris left in layers by meltwater. A moraine is formed when till is left in piles.

Write: 1. They called it "unsinkable," but the Titanic was not. They called it a floating luxury hotel, and indeed it was! It was like a grand palace, with huge rooms, gold-plated light fixtures, a swimming pool, and steam baths. No ship this big or beautiful had ever been built before. Hundreds of passengers boarded the Titanic in Southampton, England, on April 10, 1912. The great new ship was bound for New York on its maiden voyage.

At a half hour past midnight on April 15, 1912, disaster struck the Titanic. Actually, the ship struck disaster in the form of an iceberg. At first, passengers didn't realize that the accident was serious. There was a command for people to get into the lifeboats. Unfortunately, the company that built the boat was so convinced it was unsinkable that they had sent lifeboats for only about half of the people on board.

The ship sent out distress signals, hoping nearby ships would come to help. The bow of the Titanic was sinking when a loud, roaring noise went up from the ship. The Titanic was breaking apart. It stood up in the air for a short time, soon to disappear beneath the waves. The next day, another ship, the Carpathia, came to rescue 712 survivors. Hundreds more did not survive.

There are many theories about why the Titanic sank. Seventy-five years later, after much searching, the ship's wreckage was found. Small submarines have explored the wreckage. Maybe some of the mysteries of this disaster will now be solved.

2. Titles will vary.

Week 3 (pages 11–13)

MONDAY
1. third person
2. yes
3. competition
4. lift
5. yes

TUESDAY
1. Answers will vary. One possibility: Ding Meiyian hoisted 300 kg to become a women's world champion weightlifter.
2. confident
3. weightlifting
4. pneumonia, surely, wizard, chorus, physics, ghastly
5. a. Where are my new weights?
   b. Besides winning . . .
   c. Has he raised . . .
   d. She left her weights lying . . .
   e. Let me lift . . .

WEDNESDAY
1. Alex took on a task that was harder than he could handle.
2. These are the weights she lifted in today's practice: 84 kg, 66.5 kg, and 91 kg.
3. a bodybuilder's muscles
4. touch (feeling)
5. Answers will vary: Lucy is interested in the topic of strength, both inner and outer

THURSDAY
1. donkeys, pianos, O'Malleys, countries, arches, calves, volcanoes, geese
2. strongman (All other words have suffixes.)
3. defeated, caught, raised
4. A
5. Weightlifting has been around for hundreds of years dating back to ancient Greece and Egypt. It was featured in the first Modern Olympic Games in Athens, Greece in 1896. In March, 1891 the first World Weightlifting Championships were held in London, England. The International Weightlifting Federation was founded in 1905. Currently, over 160 countries participate in the organization.

FRIDAY
Read:
1. a. essay or explanation; b. joke; c. biography; d. poem; e. classified ad
2. Weightlifting competitions involve two different lifting events: the snatch and the clean & jerk.
3. d or b
4. a, c
5. clean and jerk
Write: Titles, final lines, and questions will vary.

Week 4 (pages 14–16)

MONDAY
1. d
2. them, her
3. captured, caught, escaped, robbed, worried, fought
4. yes
5. Summaries will vary: Pirates, privateers, and buccaneers all roamed the seas robbing other ships. Privateers and buccaneers had licenses for piracy, and worked under the direction of a specific country, robbing specific ships. Pirates robbed any ship for their own personal gain.

TUESDAY
1. buccaneers, tomatoes, treasures, bounties, radios, children, matches, baths
2. false
3. "Aarrr!" growled Captain Jack, "Gimme yer loot or ye'll walk the plank!"
4. robbed
5. Captions will vary.

WEDNESDAY
1. Blackbeard was a mean and dangerous man who killed many people and robbed many ships.
2. Even, Jolly, Roger
3. interrogative
4. Answers will vary: hostile, judgmental, angry
5. site = sight, caller = collar, two = too, mite = might, knead = need, pane = pain, there = their, cymbal = symbol, maid = made, medal = metal, bored = board, too = to, cent = sent, sea = see

THURSDAY
1. Descriptions and drawings will vary.
2. but
3. echo, alto, volcano, pronto, mosquitoes, mottos
4. Answers will vary; any entertainer's name will do
5. The Adventures of Peter Pan, The Curse of The Sea, The Pirate's Daughter, Pirates of the Caribbean, The Princess Bride, Treasure Island, Wolves of the Sea

FRIDAY
Read:
1. The X should be about one and a half inches directly north of Port Doubloon
2. 500 ft
3. Parrot Cove
4. 2000 ft
Write: Conversations will vary.

Week 5 (pages 17–19)

MONDAY
1. one-third, ex-boyfriend, sister-in-law
2. recite
3. b
4. opinion
5. speed, sped, will speed; choose, chose, will choose; lie, lay, will lie; take, took, will take; cheer, cheered, will cheer; win, won, will win

TUESDAY
1. exceed

2. more dangerously, most dangerously
3. lap—place where legs meet torso when sitting; lap—trip around a track or other race course
4. Cross out old and besides that.
5. Answers will vary.

WEDNESDAY
1. shrill shrieks, sudden cheers, ooohs, tire screeches, engine growls
2. Answers will vary: movable
3. plans
4. Beaseley's Race Car Repair Shop
6400 Whitewater Way
Franklin, TN 37054
April 13, 2006
Dear Mrs. Lasley:
5. She found someone to help her build the car.

THURSDAY
1. Answers will vary: sideways, outside; offhand, sendoff; downside, letdown; outrage, knockout
2. A
3. penniless, petrified
4. A
5. Answers will vary: celebratory, excited, cheerful, anticipatory

FRIDAY
Read:
1. G Force Aurora
2. 8.547 mph
3. same driver (but different cars)
4. 60 percent
5. give information about auto race speeds
6. Answers will vary. (e.g., Racers from the U.S.A. have had most of the top speeds. March-Cosworth cars are fast. Cars have not necessarily gotten faster over recent years.)
Write: Comparisons will vary.

Week 6 (pages 20–22)

MONDAY
1. a sweet liquid
2. a, b
3. cancel, bundle, terrible
4. personification, (also possibly sensory appeal)
5. in an expandable stem

TUESDAY
1. yes
2. place
3. except
4. Topic sentences will vary.
5. a. 495; c. 493; e. 494;
   b. 495; d. 496; f. 493

WEDNESDAY
1. something with four feet
2. cause: The coating a pig gets from rolling around in mud; effect: protects her from nasty insect bites and sunburn
3. If you're a bug, don't ever go near a Venus flytrap plant.
4. "Sarah, how is that tree frog able to climb up the window without sliding down?" asked Sam.
5. onomatopoeia, personification, sensory appeal

THURSDAY
1. paradox
2. tomb, gnaw, hymn, stalk
3. title, author's last name, publisher, sometimes library classification numbers
4. prepositions: during, with; objects: fights, lions
5. Answers will vary. Some possibilities:
   a. That frog fascinates me!
   b. The tree frog hangs precariously from a window.
   c. The fingers and toes appear sticky.
   d. Three frogs stick to the window now.
   e. The frog sleeps on the sunny window.

FRIDAY
Read:
1. tar = rat; tarrop = parrot; liauq = quail; woc = cow
2. to amuse the reader or challenge the reader to turn the beast's name around
3. tarrop
4. Drawings will vary; check to see that drawings include features described in the poems.
Write: Descriptions of the elidacorc will vary.

Week 7 (pages 23–25)

MONDAY
1. incidence = incidents; aisle = I'll; higher = hire; cot = caught; rite = right
2. Dr. Watson, the assistant to Sherlock Holmes, narrates the story in Doyle's well-known mystery, The Hound of the Baskervilles.
3. her
4. Answers will vary: mysterious, suspicious, strange
5. Answers will vary; one could conclude that the detective takes on a variety of cases in his business, or that the cases that he investigates are quite unusual.

TUESDAY
1. Don't tell anyone about what you heard in the hallway last night.
2. negligence, investigate, robbery, counterfeit, mystery, deceit
3. she called the police
4. Final poem lines will vary. Make sure the last word rhymes with grey.
5. 3, 6, 2, 4, 5, 1

WEDNESDAY
1. yes
2. Except for the case on Tuesday morning (the investigation of the missing tacos) the detective had a quiet week.
3. a. a clever detective; b. Slippery Sal; fingerprints on the windowsill
4. repetition, alliteration
5. Answers will vary: Someone broke into the narrator's house and vandalized it.

THURSDAY
1. investigate
2. according, restraint, forty, stolen
3. "My business was ruined!" cried the baker.
4. Answers will vary.
5. Call the emergency phone number 333–3333

FRIDAY
Read: Student reading skills for this activity will

ANSWER KEY

be determined by their answers in the writing section. Answers may vary somewhat.

Write: Theme: a mystery or strange occurrence; Tone: light-hearted and fun; Point of View: third person; Setting(s): police station, bathrooms of vacationing homeowners; Main Character: Detective Razor, a serious detective assigned to investigate strange bathtub scenes; Plot: In the town of Oak Grove, someone is entering homes while people are away and using their bathtub. (The conflict): The "serial bather" leaves a dirty bathtub and blonde hairs at the scenes of the "crimes;" police are baffled. The resolution occurs when Detective Razor, assigned to the cases, hides in the bathroom of a vacationer and catches a dog-walker letting his own dog soak in the bathtub while he does his dog-walking or pet care jobs for the vacationing homeowner.

Week 8 (pages 26–28)

MONDAY
1. Ecuador, a country whose name means "equator," is located on the equator.
2. see; place
3. home
4. d
5. Nepal is a beautiful place that Maxie wants her friend, Janelle, to see.

TUESDAY
1. volcanoes, keys, libraries, halos
2. encyclopedia, Internet
3. intrepid — cowardly
4. d
5. Titles will vary.

WEDNESDAY
1. Drop the words don't and no.
2. c
3. necessary, innocent, occur, laundry
4. Answers will vary somewhat: sandy beach, palm trees, surrounded by blue ocean water, people stranded, tropical fruit, shipwreck survivors, etc.
5. Predictions will vary. With 43 islands left to see in three days and a big storm arriving, the chances do not look good.

THURSDAY
1. "Stranded in the Costa Rican Rainforest"
2. wonderful, submersible, friendless
3. her, me
4. noun
5. Both counties border large bodies of water; both are in Central America; both border the Caribbean Sea; both are neighbors with Mexico. Guatemala is larger than Belize and has a greater population. Guatemala has more bordering neighbors. Guatemala borders the Pacific Ocean and Belize does not.

FRIDAY
Read:
1. Vatican City, Holy See
2. 28,2208
3. Haiti, Dominican Republic
4. Rwanda
5. Responses will vary.

Write: Review student descriptions to see that they contain information in the web.

Week 9 (pages 29–31)

MONDAY
1. graceful
2. Bullfighting is a popular sport in Portugal, southern France, and many Spanish-speaking countries such as Spain and Mexico.
3. Adjectives: charging, red; adverbs: skillfully
4. a
5. Examine student pictures to see that they have followed instructions.

TUESDAY
1. shortened
2. The matador ran, lept, and fell as the bull tried to gore him.
3. charging
4. bully, bumble
5. Summaries will vary.

WEDNESDAY
1. comma
2. vanquish
3. a, d
4. Answers may vary somewhat; brochure
5. Answers will vary; Observers in doorways or corners, or persons inside houses with open doors could be trampled or otherwise harmed by the bulls.

THURSDAY
1. ex
2. nonfiction
3. a. cross out here; b. cross out at; c. cross out he; d. change of to have
4. simplified, simplifying; argued, arguing; hummed, humming
5. Bullfighting is a contest between a bull and a matador. The fight begins with a trumpet fanfare and the release of the bull. The matador's helpers, called banderilleros, wave a cape to get the bull to charge. Using the cape, the matador guides the bull past his body a few times. Then picadors on horseback force lances into the bull's neck Banderilleros enter again, placing wooden sticks with sharp steel points behind the bull's neck. By the time the matador enters the ring again the bull is weakened and the matador kills it with a sword. The whole fight takes about 20 minutes.

FRIDAY
Read:
1. three
2. troubles with bulls
3. to amuse
4. Answers will vary.
5. A shy matador named Jose
   Tried to outwit a bull yesterday.
   His shoulder was torn
   By the creature's right horn,
   But the crowd just kept shouting, "Ole!"
Write: Reports will vary.

Week 10 (pages 32–34)

MONDAY
1. break, time off

2. definitely, exaggerate, almost, busy
3. nouns: summer, temperatures, corn, cobs; verbs: soared, popped
4. newcomers to the city of Southfield
5. Answers may vary somewhat; hyperbole, sensory appeal, humor

TUESDAY
1. "Pecos Bill, the greatest cowboy of all time, fell out of his family's wagon and was left behind," read the teacher to her students.
2. Change shows to show.
3. c
4. really, well
5. Answers may vary; book about tall tales or outlandish events

WEDNESDAY
1. simple subject: spider; complete predicate: has 100 legs, a gigantic forked tail, and fangs bigger than a rattlesnake's
2. Answers will vary; truth, truism, reality
3. lovely, ruder, plotted, dripping
4. alliteration
5. Any two: legends, folklore heroes, over eight feet tall, great strength, outrageous feats, special animal companion

THURSDAY
1. rein – strap for controlling animal or rein – to control, or reign – to rule over; bored – disinterested; principal – head of a school or primary; patients – clients of a doctor
2. a man's fish stories; three tall tales' titles; a scissors' handles; one family's whoppers
3. Answers may vary; Using her new camera, Susannah took a picture of a ten-foot-tall mosquito.
4. lessons, libel, lies, literal, loosely, lying
5. Headlines will vary.

FRIDAY
Read:
1. blue, horn span of 42 axe handles, can haul great quantities of wood, eats 30 lb. of grain a day
2. 108,000 calories
3. Great Lakes
4. Answers will vary.
Write: Articles will vary.

Week 11 (pages 35–37)

MONDAY
1. a
2. Seventy-five percent of pet owners—you may not believe this—sign their pet's name to their greeting cards.
3. Answers will vary (catfish, catnap, bookwork, earthworm, bluebird, blackbird, doghouse)
4. 5
5. a snake's home in a terrarium

TUESDAY
1. in a math book
2. eludes
3. a
4. Phrases will vary; check for sensory appeal.
5. one-third

WEDNESDAY
1. You can expect to pay a high price for a macaw.
2. c
3. elegant, pheasant, elephant, apparent
4. b. c
5. A dog named Brutus is a sky diver.

THURSDAY
1. Prudel the parrot knew 800 English words. Her favorite sentence was, "What are you doing?"
2. kids
3. animated
4. subject
5. The writer shows a bias against the idea of expensive pet weddings. Conclusions will vary.

FRIDAY
Read:
1. to give information about pets
2. prospective pet owners or other people interested in rats and ferrets
3. Answers will vary: needs time to run around, name means "little thief," hides things, does not get along with other small animals, quiet, can be trained to use a litter box, has distinct personality
4. Answers will vary: fits into small cage, smart, social, cute, food easy to obtain
5. Answers will vary. Ferret: needs time to run around, hides things, doesn't get along with other small animals; Rat: active at night, short life span
Write: Arguments will vary.

Week 12 (pages 38–40)

MONDAY
1. c
2. failure, vacation, explosion
3. tale of a cowboy
4. gnat (g); knickers (k); edges (d); scheme (h); wriggle (w); gourmet (t)
5. a. no; b. about 72,000,000

TUESDAY
1. Capitalize all words except a; underline or italicize the title, add an apostrophe before the s in Disneys, add a colon or a dash after parade.
2. of electricity, to any part, of the house
3. a flash of light produced by the movement of electricity between two clouds or from a cloud to the earth
4. electronic music
5. Most people have experienced an electric charge. It happens when you walk across a carpet and touch a metal doorknob, or when you take off a wool cap and your hair stands on end. All matter has atoms. All atoms contain electrically charged particles (protons and electrons). When they are rubbed, electrons jump from one object to another, causing a charge.

WEDNESDAY
1. tattoos, ferries, tablespoons, glasses, mice, fathers-in-law, canopies, cellos, superheroes
2. yes
3. One power plant provided electricity for 160,000 homes; another produced

electricity for fewer than 100,000 homes. (OR, example may be two complete sentences, with period after homes and capital A on another.)
4. The writer stereotypes all people who get power from other sources as antisocial or hostile to social institutions.
5. F, O, F, O, F, F, O

THURSDAY
1. Change uses to used.
2. zenith
3. negligence, evidence, occurrence, acceptance, abundance, absence
4. a thesaurus
5. Topic sentences will vary.

FRIDAY
Read:
Across 3. train
4. speakers
5. fan
7. ships
8. toaster
9. cell phone
12. spa
13. TV
14. calculator
16. drill
Down 1. jet ski
2. microscope
5. flashlight
6. iron
8. treadmill
10. elevator
11. electrify
15. chip
Write: Joke completions will vary.

Week 13 (pages 41–43)

MONDAY
1. Antonyms will vary; samples: scrawny – brawny; boisterous – quiet; adroit – clumsy; parsimonious – generous; punctual – tardy; sensitive – callous
2. "My friend Moe does exactly the opposite of everything I do," said Joe.
3. tone
4. exclamatory
5. Predictions will vary.

TUESDAY
1. evening, morning, brilliant, shadowy, moderate, extreme
2. Linking verbs: is, is; Predicate adjectives: pliable, brittle
3. all have similar meanings
4. Cross out it, most, another waterfall called
5. Answers may vary somewhat. Eiffel Tower is 900 feet taller; Tower of Pisa is leaning; Tower of Pisa is round, and the Eiffel Tower is triangular in space.

WEDNESDAY
1. b, d
2. opposites
3. altercation—quarrel; vigilant—watchful; convene—gather
4. skating, stopped, lovely
5. 4, 5, 1, 3, 2

THURSDAY
1. crooked, fast, found, lost, narrow, slow, straight, wide

2. Scarcely any animal is as tall as a giraffe, but don't worry any about feeling sorry for that short beetle. He has a powerful sting.
3. no
4. Antarctica, quite, opposite, Africa, icy, covered, thick, forests
5. Revisions will vary.
   a. When Mike and Tyson jumped from the hot tub into a snowbank, (they OR Mike OR Tyson) shouted, "Yikes!"
   b. While I was dreaming about skydiving and scuba diving, the telephone started ringing.
   c. Mice ran across our tent floor while we were telling stories about the best and worst moments of the day.

FRIDAY
Read:
1. The first and last lines name opposites. (They are also one-word lines.)
2. waking, moving, bustling, yawning, slowing, quieting
3. Line 3 has words builds an energetic feeling with words that speed up to fast movements; Line 5 has words that are slowing things down with a sleepy feel.
4. dusk
Write: Poems will vary. Check to see that they follow the form as outlined in the instructions.

Week 14 (pages 44–46)

MONDAY
1. alliteration
2. pillow, mummy, ten, wife, valuable, dignitary
3. c
4. The Great Sphinx is an amazing structure to see.
5. mourn – morn; bury – berry; vial – vile; carat – carrot or caret; hear – here; creak – creek; reign – rain or rein

TUESDAY
1. colon (or dash)
2. death
3. common: lifeblood, soil, river, setting, food supply
   proper: Nile River, Egypt
4. no
5. Summaries will vary: Because Egyptians believed in an afterlife, they preserved bodies and prepared tombs with supplies for continuing life.

WEDNESDAY
1. fancier, lied, finally, likeable
2. gerund
3. expository
4. showed
5. Check student drawings to see that they have followed directions correctly.

THURSDAY
1. a dictionary
2. What's the most interesting fact you've learned about the Egyptians' culture?
3. friendless
4. the Egyptians were able to develop a calendar
5. Topic sentences will vary.

ANSWER KEY

FRIDAY
Read:
1. The body is covered with a mud pack of natron and dried for 40 days.
2. natron
3. Answers will vary. (Step 5)
4. Answers will vary.
5. Removal of internal organs, saving them in jars.
Write: Beginnings will vary.

Week 15 (pages 47–49)

MONDAY
1. "What could explain the disappearance of a whole village?" Joe Labelle wondered when he discovered that all 2,000 people were gone.
2. the disappearance of all 2,000 people in a village
3. a. the village's disappearance;
   b. the searchers' questions;
   c. five searchers' journey;
   d. one searcher's questions.
4. illusion
5. b, c, e

TUESDAY
1. into the Bermuda Triangle
2. tropical, hysterical, candle
3. mysterious happenings, sometimes dangerous or criminal, people searching, lots of questions
4. c
5. Questions will vary.

WEDNESDAY
1. a. against; b. thousand; c. across; d. beyond
2. Dr. J. Allen Hynek, an astronomer consultant to the U.S. Air Force, formed a long, precise definition of a UFO.
3. comparative = better; superlative = best
4. sailors, tourists, passengers, boat owners, or anyone else who has any connections to travel across this area
5. Paraphrases will vary. Make sure students include the essential ideas of the paragraph.

THURSDAY
1. It is good that you saw that UFO when it landed. You reacted well by reporting it.
2. index
3. yacht
4. light on the field = set down;
   flashing lights = electrical appliances that give off light;
   light up the sky = brighten
5. Some people claim that green flashes are just a myth—that you can never see one. They are real; but they are rare. A green flash occurs at sunset when the sun suddenly changes color from red to blue and, for a few seconds, looks green. A brief ray of green appears to shoot up from the horizon, giving the impression of a green flash. This happens only in the middle latitudes under specific atmospheric conditions. Most people who look for green flashes are not lucky enough to see them

FRIDAY
Read:
1. report or article
2. to inform
3. no
4. a ship, the U.S.S. Cyclops
Write: Stories will vary. Check to be sure that each student's story does fit with the items and events in the picture.

Week 16 (pages 50–52)

MONDAY
1. plot
2. A luxury steamboat, The American Queen
3. Yours truly, Hoyt D. Sayle
4. Antonyms and synonyms will vary.
5. A hydrofoil is a ship that can move faster than other ships because it skims the water instead of moving through it.

TUESDAY
1. no
2. most = adverb; force = noun; drives = verb; into = preposition; suction = noun
3. b
4. memos, defies, sopranos
5. Titles will vary.

WEDNESDAY
1. On November 9, 2001, Omar Hanapiev pulled a 1,269,861-pound ship with his teeth.
2. a. adjective; b. verb; c. noun
3. The captain scolded or harshly criticized the crew member.
4. expository writing
5. 3, 6, 7, 2, 5, 4, 1

THURSDAY
1. currant, surf, waive, weighed, holey, sale
2. no
3. 100 section
4. fight, sit, go, sing, take, raise, lie, leave
5. The edit may vary some, depending upon how writers correct the grammatical and structural errors. Here is one possibility: A legendary ship is at the center of a fascinating ghost story. The Flying Dutchman is a phantom ship that was on a trip around Africa's Cape of Good Hope. According to the story, the captain had a crew of dead men. Because of some curse on him or the ship, the Dutchman sails forever, never reaching its port. This mysterious ship has become the subject of many pieces of literature and music, including Samuel Coleridge's poem, "The Rime of the Ancient Mariner".

FRIDAY
Read: The diamond could be in any of these places: the Galley, Cockpit, Aft Deck, or on the stairway
Write: Conclusions will vary.

Week 17 (pages 53–55)

MONDAY
1. The gulper eel's tail is like a whip; its mouth is wide and deep like a pelican's.
2. fragment
3. pursuer or attacker
4. This salmon will return to its home stream.
5. a, b, c

TUESDAY
1. mine, ours, his, theirs
2. Answers will vary. The sperm whale dives to a depth of 10,000 feet.
3. sworn, swordplay, syllable, synonym, symptom
4. wouldn't, it'll, we're, could've
5. a. fish; b. corm; c. worm; d. board; box; head

WEDNESDAY
1. I Was Slimed By An Atlantic Hagfish
2. Inferences will vary. The person might be a deep sea diver.
3. irrationality
4. participial: looking fierce; prepositional: from his nostrils
5. aabbcccc

THURSDAY
1. Of all the animals on Earth, the blue whale is the largest. Of all the animals on Earth, blue whales are the largest.
2. The longest fish migration on record was a trip by a blue fin tuna. The fish traveled 5,800 miles from Baja, California, Mexico, to the sea south of Tokyo, Japan.
3. locate
4. ocean fish
5. Revisions will vary. Look for variety in sentence structure and combination of short sentences.

FRIDAY
Read:
1. to entertain or amuse
2. 1
3. I will feel out of place swimming with the guppies.
4. eat
5. If you eat that worm, you will be hooked on a fishhook and be caught by some human.
Write: Revisions may vary. Here are some possibilities:
1. Since we were cold and weary from a long day of fishing, the fire on the beach looked good to us.
2. When Todd was loaded up with his gear getting onto the boat, he saw a swordfish.
3. Bob and his fishing buddies heard on the radio the news about a storm coming.
4. I settled into a comfortable spot and used my new fishing pole to catch a fish.
5. The proud fishermen served the catch smothered in onions to their wives.
6. The fisherman's green vest fell off the pier.
7. After the fishing trip, we invited our friend Joe to join us for dinner.
8. While I was relaxing in my boat, several fish jumped at least a foot.

Week 18 (pages 56–58)

MONDAY
1. Is it true that more movies are made in India than in any other country?
2. personification
3. dislike
4. stereos, theaters, patches, beliefs, mouthfuls, clothes, axes, crises
5. a. It has broken all records for earnings; b. about $780 million

TUESDAY
1. quotes of significance
2. heirloom—h; gnash—g; muscle—c; pledge—d; thyme—h; balmy—l
3. inordinate
4. er, ent, or, ant, ar, ist
5. a. G; b. PR; c. I; d. G; e. PA

WEDNESDAY
1. assure
2. b
3. outrageous, jealous, anonymous, dangerous, gorgeous, suspicious
4. onomatopoeia
5. a. F; b. O; c. O; d. F; e. F

THURSDAY
1. Spanish-speaking
2. obtuse – sharp
3. past
4. *Pirates of the Caribbean: The Curse of the Back Pearl* is the top-earning pirate film. This followed other popular pirate movies such as *Hook, Peter Pan,* and *Shipwrecked.*
5. yes

FRIDAY
Read: Drawings will vary. Check to see that the drawings are reasonable outcomes of reading the captions.
Write: Captions will vary. Check to see that they fit reasonably with the pictures.

Week 19 (pages 59–61)

MONDAY
1. because
2. airborne
3. d
4. two-thirds, son-in-law, forty-two
5. A balloon is propelled by air pressure that forces air out the opening.

TUESDAY
1. This airplane has hardly any space between the seats.
2. atmosphere, barometer, molecules, separate, propel, fight
3. station air = play or run; hot air = atmospheric gas
4. aerial, aerodynamic, airline, airplane, airport
5. It appears that several rockets are needed.

WEDNESDAY
1. praise
2. action verbs: take, land linking verb: is
3. Greater air pressure on the outside of the can.
4. "London's Heathrow Airport is the busiest international airport in the world," Britta told me. (OR Britta told me, "London's Heathrow Airport is the busiest international airport in the world.")
5. a, d

THURSDAY
1. learn about or figure out
2. conceited, sheik
3. the rockets that launch the space shuttle
4. Topic sentence: The Gossamer Albatross is a special aircraft built to be powered by human muscles.
5. The bicycle is enclosed in a thin shell.

FRIDAY
Read: Check completed airplanes to see that they are crafted as directed.
Write: Descriptive words, phrases, and similes will vary.

Week 20 (pages 62–64)

MONDAY
1. semicolon
2. complex
3. separate
4. b
5. the oldest son of the second son or, if there are no sons, the eldest daughter of the second son

TUESDAY
1. no
2. taste, preference
3. applaud, dread, neurotic, broil
4. Her Majesty, Queen Elizabeth II, ascended to the throne on February 6, 1952, upon the death of her father, King George VI.
5. light

WEDNESDAY
1. legend = noun; fought = verb; valiantly = adverb; against = preposition
2. notoriety
3. Capitalize: She, Sundays, St, Patrick's, Day, Easter, Bastille Day, Thanksgiving
4. The queen took a risk to bestow knighthood on me.
5. Answers will vary. Students might draw a conclusion that there is some possibility Arthur did exist.

THURSDAY
1. hear—here; knight—night; seize—sees or seas
2. victories, grandchildren, clashes, horses, swords, castles
3. Adorned in the finest gold crown and velvet robe, the queen rode in a carriage.
4. meanings, histories, pronunciations, parts of speech
5. two years

FRIDAY
Read:
1. Check to see that graphs are done correctly.
2. Queen Victoria
3. 38 yeats
Write: Explanations will vary.

Week 21 (pages 65–67)

MONDAY
1. to see or look at or examine
2. b
3. innocence, persistence
4. persuasive (possible narrative)
5. Answers will vary.

TUESDAY
1. yes
2. careful to do things correctly
3. Claude Monet, the great impressionist painter, was born in Paris, France on November 14, 1840.
4. Salvador Dali, Edgar Degas, Vincent van Gogh, Claude Monet, Pablo Picasso, Andrew Wyeth
5. Paragraphs will vary somewhat.

WEDNESDAY
1. exaggerate, exception, expiration, excess, excuses, complexion
2. exclude
3. those, that
4. c, d
5. Conclusions may vary: The prices indicate that they are fairly inexperienced.

THURSDAY
1. nonfiction
2. The sculpture was very expensive.
3. It took 25,297 painters three years, two months to complete the painting, "A Little Dab of Texas."
4. blockhead, nose
5. Titles and conclusions will vary.

FRIDAY
Read:
1. poetry
2. sharp crimson spikes shoot like arrows
3. fuchsia fragments fling themselves; yellows sparkle, stretching their wiggly fingers out to claw at the skies
4. lines 4, 6, 7, 8
5. lines 7, 12, 13
Write: Poems will vary.

Week 22 (pages 68–70)

MONDAY
1. yes
2. in = not; hyper = over or above; retro = backwards
3. H.C. Harris will whistle at the same time that he will play a harmonica with his nose.
4. The writer believes Dr. Vargas should not have fled his country, but should have stayed and become president.
5. Answers will vary. Similarities: Both address the same topic. Both give some information about Dr. Vargas. Differences: The passages are different forms (article or story and poem); the poem is shorter, the article gives more information, one is prose and the other is poetry, the poem expresses an opinion while the article is neutral, one rhymes.

TUESDAY
1. European, Chicago, Halloween, Antarctica
2. dairy
3. The connotation of *grab* is *to take hold of quickly in order to get something fast. Seize* has a more urgent, aggressive connotation—that of taking something forcefully, or taking something that does not belong to you.
4. 110
5. Believe It or Not! When a woman from Collingwood, Australia lost her voice for a long time, she hoped it would return. But she never imagined how it would return! An accident caused the loss of Ellen Matther's voice. Seven and one-half years later, her voice returned with a Scottish accent. She was Australian, not Scottish!

WEDNESDAY
1. Pendl's
2. outrageous, unbelievable
3. prepositions: of, by; phrases: of some

ANSWER KEY

important minerals (calcium, phosphorous, iron) and by eating 20 caterpillars
4. abcb
5. Summaries will vary somewhat. A dog rescued 92 passengers from a shipwreck by swimming to shore with a lifeline.

THURSDAY
1. jealousy, symptoms
2. reject—repudiate, deceit—treachery
3. A company in Japan produces false fingernails
4. title, author's name, illustrator's name, publisher, location of publisher
5. sobering

FRIDAY
Read:
1. They all involve water dangers and survivals.
2. The chocolate snow or the shipwreck
3. 250,000,000
4. The snow might have only looked like chocolate.
5. Answers will vary.
Write: Letters will vary. Check to see that structure and mechanics follow proper form for a friendly letter.

Week 23 (pages 71–73)
MONDAY
1. w in wraps; the first l in calmly; h in chord, d in ledge; b in climbs
2. Compounds will vary. Here are a few possibilities: headstrong, headache, headway, headphones, headband, headlight, arrowhead, letterhead, hothead, figurehead, thunderhead, hardhead
3. single, tiny, armored, giant, eight
4. why spiders weave webs
5. A Greek myth tells the story of Arachne, a young girl who challenged the goddess Athena and was changed into a spider. The girl and her descendents were doomed to spend eternity weaving and hanging from threads.

TUESDAY
1. Answers will vary.
2. pretended
3. Topic sentences will vary.
4. Australia's most famous poisonous spider (the Sydney funnel-web spider) has not caused any deaths in recent years.
5. It is likely that the teenager will have pain and discomfort, but will not die.

WEDNESDAY
1. toxic
2. anybody, several, either, some, all, none
3. dangerous, instead
4. to amuse or entertain
5. Inferences will vary; People may be frightened by the possibility of danger, even if there is none. Or, they may be frightened by the quick movement or appearance of the spiders.

THURSDAY
1. count spiders—determine the number or amount; doesn't count—matter
2. Why does the black widow female eat the male after mating? Is it because he snores

so badly?
3. all of these
4. Revisions will vary. (With its long legs and amazing strength, the Goliath birdeater tarantula snatches a bird right out of its nest.)
5. Professor J. Mite
   Department of Zoology
   Chicago University
   Chicago, IL 60606
   April 4, 2005
   Dear Professor Mite:
   I would like to take a course that studies arachnids. Can you make a suggestion of where I might find such a course?
   Yours truly,
   Chester C. Webbs

FRIDAY
Read:
1. to stun their prey
2. Fred
3. guess
4. They carry venom to stun their prey, only 25 species are harmful to humans, a Goliath tarantula can be 11 inches wide
5. That's 25 too many! I have arachnaphobia! Eeeeek! (although this is not a sentence)
Write: Conversations will vary. Check to see that dialogues are correctly capitalized and punctuated.

Week 24 (pages 74–76)
MONDAY
1. On a trip to see some of the biggest swamps in the United States, Sophie saw the Dismal Swamp, the Okefenokee Swamp, and the Everglades.
2. tundra (or forest)
3. veto, watch, teeth, cactus, measles, wolf, ox, penny
4. a
5. development and the straightening of the river

TUESDAY
1. lazily, out
2. Southern, Florida, alligators, crocodiles, habitat
3. abnormal, overspend
4. nonfiction
5. Descriptions will vary.

WEDNESDAY
1. onomatopoeia
2. dangerous
3. "How to Get Out of An Alligator's Grip"
4. Why are you taking a trip to the Dismal Swamp? You will surely put yourself into danger unnecessarily.
5. Check drawings to see that student has followed the directions.

THURSDAY
1. George was in a difficult situation when he fell off a dock into the jaws of an alligator.
2. Snakes, opossums, foxes, bears, Swamp, Carolina, Virginia
3. a. a crocodile's jaws; b. three alligators' bites
4. Omit here; change shows to show.
5. Revisions will vary.

a. Which crocodile snaps his jaws?
b. Mort wrestles an alligator.
c. Three angry crocs are chasing your boat.
d. That one can devour your arm in a minute.

FRIDAY
Read:
1. lighthearted
2. They are both about alligator bites. They are both prose. They both have a similar mood and tone.
3. all ages
4. trying
5. quite a lot
Write: Preventions and cures will vary.

Week 25 (pages 77–79)
MONDAY
1. panther
2. also – adverb; is – verb; hollow – noun; enough – adverb; enter – verb
3. sure, it'll, cave's, interior, carefully, because, slippery
4. simile
5. a. the action of underground water
   b. moving water
   c. surf pounds on rocks along the shore
   d. the roof of a cave collapses

TUESDAY
1. best
2. definitions of terms used in the book
3. Today, Grandpa Smith led a group of 20 German tourists on a tour of Crystal Cave.
4. plumb, probe, scrutinize
5. Details will vary. The detail needs to be something that transitions from the classroom discussion to the actual trip.

WEDNESDAY
1. Brad and I; come along with him and me
2. angelic, childlike, magical
3. friends, neighbors, risky, hobby, easy, taking, difficult, expedition
4. Predictions will vary. Due to lack of concern about safety, the business may fail, or may be the subject of lawsuits.
5. persuasive

THURSDAY
1. gerund
2. Bats have a scary reputation. They are not particularly harmful to humans, however.
3. do – dew; not – knot; prints – prince
4. Flint Ridge Cave, National Park Service, Echo River
5. Echo River

FRIDAY
Read:
1. 1, 2, 3, 4, 5, 6, 7, 8
2. sturdy boots or shoes, layers of clothing with waterproof outer layer, helmet
3. The hike out is often uphill, so it is harder. Also, it is the end of the day and hikers are likely to be tired and cold—with less energy.
4. The trip might take longer than planned; cavers might get lost or stranded; lights that seem reliable might burn out more quickly than planned.
Write: Instructions should read something like this: Head straight out of the Emerald

Room (south) until you hit the end of the trail. Turn left (east) onto Rainbow Bridge Walk. Curve left (north) into Echo Cavern. Follow the trail left (northwest) out of Echo Cavern. Turn right (east) into Stalactite Corridor. Do not take any turns until you hit the end of the corridor. Turn right (south) and follow the trail into Painted Chamber. Turn left (south) toward the Exit.

Week 26 (pages 80–82)

MONDAY
1. a. who; b.Who's; c. Whoever
2. My question is this: Who pays the dog's credit card bills?
3. adept
4. a California forest
5. Summaries will vary: A Search and Rescue dog tracked and found a lost girl by following the smell of her skin cells.

TUESDAY
1. regretting, hoping, fussing, robbing, begging, supplying
2. he
3. bombardier
4. Antonyms will vary: Do not Irritate the Animals.
5. – A flock of sparrows in New Zealand learned to open the automatic doors of a bus station.
   – A dog named Brutus has a busy skydiving career.
   – A Northern pine snake has the amazing ability to swallow and breathe at the same time.
   – An African grasshopper blows bitter, bad-smelling bubbles when danger is near.
   – The bombardier beetle scalds its enemies by spraying boiling liquid.

WEDNESDAY
1. "Did you know," asked Luke, "that a longhorn bull named Merril was trained to star in a TV commercial?"
2. graceful
3. expository
4. c
5. Impressions will vary.

THURSDAY
1. Revisions will vary.
2. spotted dog – blotched or dotted; spotted a train – saw
3. peculiar, original, baboon, interrupt
4. They identify the part of speech for each definition.
5. a, b, e

FRIDAY
Read:
1. three
2. collie, horse, ferret, elephants
3. Answers will vary.
Write: Titles and couplets will vary.

Week 27 (pages 83–85)

MONDAY
1. fragment
2. Answers will vary: football, footwear, footbridge, footbath, footstool, footlocker
3. rose, went, thought, was, bought, rang,

went, lost
4. point of view
5. 7-year old hired as a consultant and win of dance championship

TUESDAY
1. This biography of Paul McCartney is just the kind of thing I like.
2. Twelve-year old Jennifer Capriati's win of a Wimbledon tennis match changed everyone's view of her.
3. twelve-year old Billy Gilman didn't expect to sell a million copies.
4. no
5. Revisions may vary somewhat. Amadeus Wolfgang Mozart was a prodigy. At age five, Mozart was composing music. By age 13, he was presenting concerts throughout Europe and had written several difficult pieces of music, including symphonies. Although he is now regarded as one of the most important composers in history, he died in poverty at age 35.

WEDNESDAY
1. biography = write; automotive = move; inedible = eat
2. Africa, donated, blood, consecutive
3. no
4. a
5. Answers may vary. They both participate in events that take great physical ability. They both accomplished feats no one else had—at the youngest age for the feat. There is a nine year difference in their ages at the time of their accomplishments. Tara participates in an organized sport. Andrew's event was witnessed by fewer people.

THURSDAY
1. celebrated = past; love = present
2. Jonathan wanted to read biographies of astronauts, drummers, presidents, firefighters, and skateboarders.
3. a gazetteer
4. amateur
5. Topic Sentences will vary.

FRIDAY
Read:
1. biography
2. to inform readers about the lives of two people
3. The both were the first to accomplish something.
4. 872 hours
5. Eileen commanded a space shuttle mission; Lance won his seventh Tour de France.
Write: Sentences will vary.

Week 28 (pages 86–88)

MONDAY
1. warm
2. United, States, America, Hawaiian, Islands, Ka Lae
3. hot, dry
4. sense of touch
5. 7, 4, 2, 6, 3, 5, 1, 8

TUESDAY
1. nickname
2. Louisiana, special, distinction, Capital

3. Revisions will vary.
4. Introductions will vary.
5. United States – 1703; unison – 1703, underdog – 1700, unfit – 1702

WEDNESDAY
1. imperative
2. direct objects – name; indirect – glacier
3. infamous – well-known for something disgraceful or unpleasant; odious – bad-smelling
4. Sentences will vary.
5. decaying plant matter used as fertilizer for the mushrooms

THURSDAY
1. exploring, plopping, hurrying, echoing, shoveling, suspecting, wishing, voting
2. week – weak; beaches – beeches; clothes – close; idle – idol; days – daze; pale – pail; sun – son; coral – choral; your – you're
3. They are organized according to general categories. These categories and sub-categories are assigned numbers or letters in a library system such as the Dewey Decimal System or the Library of Congress system.
4. Titles will vary.
5. Check – verb; good – adjective; they – pronoun; industry – noun; because – conjunction; Chinese – adjective; continually – adverb; imports – noun.

FRIDAY
Read:
Maps will vary, depending upon state. Check for accuracy.
Write: Paragraphs will vary.

Week 29 (pages 89–91)

MONDAY
1. in, for
2. They all have suffixes.
3. lady, sued, salon, treatment, thousand, dollar, settlement
4. stereotyping
5. Answers will vary.

TUESDAY
1. pleasing, smooth
2. U.S., Supreme, Court's, Miranda, Arizona, Brown, Board, Education
3. to segregate
4. to inform about the purpose and activities of the Supreme Court
5. Arguments will vary.

WEDNESDAY
1. illicit
2. Ruth Bader Ginsberg, the second woman to serve on the U.S. Supreme Court, was appointed to her position in 1993.
3. Revisions will vary; The defendant brought his lawyer a check wrapped in a brown envelope.
4. Amanda swallowed a cockroach along with her soup and threatened to sue the restaurant (or the manager).
5. a–b–c–b–d–e–f–e–e

THURSDAY
1. advice
2. the act of putting something to proof

ANSWER KEY

3. c, d
4. Titles will vary.
5. a. Tennessee — lassoing fish;
   b. Memphis — frogs croaking

FRIDAY
Read:
1. Belinda Bleet
2. both involve problems with neighbors; both ask for pain and suffering compensation
3. person bringing the lawsuit
4. Cases Two and Three
5. Mr. Port (his name); Belinda Bleet (goat owner) Olive family (name); neighbors "green" with envy
Write: Outlines may vary somewhat but should have the three cases as the main categories with factors from each case listed below the main points.

Week 30 (pages 92–94)

MONDAY
1. patience, patients
2. no
3. tone
4. He is eating; She ate; He will eat
5. Check drawings.

TUESDAY
1. prosecuted
2. The cook at Bubba's, by the way, claimed that is was all a joke
3. subjective
4. a quotation index or the Internet
5. The Ninja Burger Company was founded in 1954. It is an unusual food service, run by ninjas. Supposedly, employees deliver fresh, hot food to special customers. The trouble is, everything is top secret, so no one knows who the customers are or whether the service actually exists.

WEDNESDAY
1. invention, decision
2. a. the sauce's flavor;
   b. many meatballs' spices;
   c. several cooks' hats;
   c. a menu's choices
3. enjoyable – able to be; liquefy – to make; flavorful – full of; baker – one who
4. metaphor
5. Headlines and conclusions will vary.

THURSDAY
1. someone who enjoys food a lot
2. semicolon: cafe; they...
3. Eating at Lynn's Paradise Café
4. piquant
5. Answers will vary somewhat: Beasey's Burgers, Chez Henri, Mama's Bakery, Natural Cafe, Pasta-A-Plenty, Raja's Cuisine, Ray's Hot Dogs, Sue's Subs, Tasty Cone, Taste of Thai, Wraps & More

FRIDAY
Read:
1. fifty
2. minestrone (zuppa)
3. fruit of the sea-fish
4. fresh sliced mozzarella, basil, tomatoes
5. distracted by being in love
Write: Predictions and conclusions will vary.

Week 31 (pages 95–97)

MONDAY
1. compound
2. know, pitch
3. Don't get mad because you can't figure out how to work the bicycle.
4. second person
5. one of the holes in the metal plate (containing a gumball) lining up with the slot that leads to the outer door

TUESDAY
1. Sears Tower, Norwegian, American Clock Company
2. each, big, city, bright, neon – five
3. glowing, full of light
4. neon, nerd, neither
5. Revisions will vary.

WEDNESDAY
1. negligent, heedless
2. burning in the toaster
3. invisible, reversible
4. b
5. O, F, F, O, O

THURSDAY
1. Garage door openers are not sold there either.
2. a. antigerms;
   b. mistake;
   c. cooperate
3. When the light from a smoke detector bounces off smoke, it reflects back to hit a photocell. This activates an alarm.
4. Summaries will vary; The heat of a fire rises to the sprinkler heads, breaks a seal, and allows water to spray out. Some of the water triggers an alarm.
5. Water which escapes through a side valve and spins a wheel.

FRIDAY
Read:
1. It takes thousands of people to make a pencil; no one person can do it.
2. essay or article
3. No, it is made of graphite.
4. rubber trees in Malaysia
Write: Lists will vary.

Week 32 (pages 98–100)

MONDAY
1. peculiar, scandalous, preposterous, jealous
2. They had an argument.
3. b, c
4. The writer doesn't believe in the idea of time traveling.
5. H.G. Wells wrote a story in which a man builds a time machine and tells his friends that he traveled ahead into time.

TUESDAY
1. despicable (Answers may vary.)
2. yes
3. This is an interesting idea: wormholes are tunnels through time and space.
4. b, c, d
5. Revisions will vary.

WEDNESDAY
1. "Are you sure," asked Jake, "that a black hole is a gateway to other universes?"
2. Answers will vary. The answer must be a compound word that begins with worm, such as wormhole.
3. How exciting!
4. Evaluations will vary.
5. a. pun; b. simile; c. personification

THURSDAY
1. present, present
2. participial
3. convenient, neighbors, shriek
4. The Table of Contents is at the beginning of the book; it lists the general topics of the book in the order they appear. The Index is at the back and is more extensive. It lists detailed topics in alphabetical order. Both give page numbers.
5. Details will vary.

FRIDAY
Read:
1. Answers may vary; *Time Machines*, *Space Time Physics*, *Black Holes, Wormholes, & Time Machines*, *How to Build A Time Machine*
2. *Space Time Physics*
3. *A Wind in the Door and A Wrinkle in Time*
4. *The Ancient One*
Write: Completed sentences will vary.

Week 33 (pages 101–103)

MONDAY
1. parentheses around (that's the world's highest volcano)
2. climax
3. denotation
4. cause: violent currents from steep falls; effect: carving out of a deep, round basin
5. a. IM;   c. IN;   e. IM;
   b. D;   d. D;   f. E

TUESDAY
1. Canyon, donkeys, bottom
2. carry
3. Bob and Lou shouldn't have tried to climb up Machu Picchu alone.
4. biographical dictionary
5. Answers may vary.
   interrogative = whatever, which;
   possessive = ours, hers;
   singular = it;
   demonstrative = that;
   plural = ours, both;
   indefinite = somebody, some

WEDNESDAY
1. to place emphasis on the word long
2. Peru's main tourist attraction
3. a. straight, strait;
   b. crews, cruise
4. Gateway Arch, Space Needle
5. Inferences will vary.

THURSDAY
1. similar meanings
2. Change *among* to *between*
3. damaged, conquer, ruins
4. c
5. Prose versions will vary.

FRIDAY
Read:
1. five
2. 69–72, four pages
3. Niagara Falls, Mammoth Caves,

Grand Canyon
4. pages 84–85
Write: Postcards will vary.

Week 34 (pages 104–106)

MONDAY
1. name and address of sender; name and address of person to whom letter is written, date
2. Every = adjective; faithfully = adverb; objects = noun
3. pretender
4. hyperbole
5. sunglasses and hats

TUESDAY
1. difficult
2. desert
3. linking = is; action = found
4. garish
5. the ski hat

WEDNESDAY
1. down
2. searching, searched, marrying, married, echoing, echoed, stubbing, stubbed, matching, matched
3. a
4. metaphor
5. a. alarming the citizens
   b. the whale is confused;
   c. whales turn up in strange places;
   d. officials ran into the water to push the whale back to deeper water

THURSDAY
1. Ellen McFaul, Disneyland's
2. enlighten, clarify, explain
3. In January of 2006, a lost whale swam up the River Thames in Central London.
4. Replace good with well. Replace whom with who.
5. 6, 5, 4, 1, 3, 2, 7

FRIDAY
Read:
1. Answers will vary.
2. Answers will vary.
Write: Ads will vary.

Week 35 (pages 107–109)

MONDAY
1. Tunes to Match Your Hula-Hooping
2. have sold more than a billion discs and tapes
3. ran away with, stole
4. personification
5. 6, 4, 1, 3, 2, 5 or 6, 5, 1, 3, 2, 4

TUESDAY
1. a. Why do you like hip-hop music?;
   b. Where is the drummer?
2. biodegradable, brontosaurus
3. music or percussion
4. Grammy
5. Revisions will vary.

WEDNESDAY
1. flout
2. Isn't, band's
3. imagery
4. a. screeching – gerund;
   b. drumming – gerund;

c. spinning – participle;
d. to stop – infinitive
5. Hula hooping is coming back into fashion, inspired by one band's gimmick. Adults are the ones participating this time, spinning bigger hoops.

THURSDAY
1. rowdy
2. hits
3. nonfiction or biography
4. guitar, popularity, quartet, auditorium, microphone, management
5. Captions will vary.

FRIDAY
Read:
1. Libra Music Co
2. Answers will vary.
3. Kelly
4. B.B.
Write: Descriptive words and phrases will vary.

Week 36 (pages 110–112)

MONDAY
1. a. linking;
   b. action;
   c. action
   d. linking
2. business, restaurant, nuisance
3. fiction, make-believe
4. hyperbole
5. Inferences will vary.

TUESDAY
1. outlandish, impossible
2. no
3. Answers will vary; Mermaids caught the attention of sailors by sitting on the rocks, singing, and combing their hair.
4. Answers will vary.
5. • Is there any truth to the stories about mermaids?
   • I hear that tales of mermaids are universal; who was first to tell them?
   • Are mermaids always female? Aren't there any males?
   • Has anyone seen the sculpture of the mermaid in Copenhagen Harbor?
   • Is it true that mermaids washed up in Malaysia after the 2004 tsunami?

WEDNESDAY
1. Will is staying up late and getting up early to read about Atlantis.
2. h in schedule, w in wrestler, h in chorus, g in gnash, d in budge, p in pseudonym
3. yes
4. a. true; b. true
5. The manatees share some characteristics with the mermaid descriptions: cradling babies, "hair", coming up from the sea, big tail, basking on rocks

THURSDAY
1. marina – sea; geology – earth; durable – hard; cryptic – secret
2. Mermaids, legendary aquatic creatures, seem to be part fish and part human.
3. periodicals
4. prepositional

5. Answers will vary. The movie, *Splash*, tells the story of a mermaid who fell in love with a human. When she is on dry land, the mermaid looks normal. When any water is splashed on her legs, they change into a fishtail. The movie revolves around her efforts to keep her boyfriend from learning that she is a mermaid.

FRIDAY
Write: Revisions/corrections may vary. In particular, students may correct grammatical usage errors differently.

For centuries, people have been fascinated with Plato's tales about the legendary continent of Atlantis. Plato, a writer in ancient Greece, wove a tale of a great empire that existed on an island continent. According to him, this was a brilliant civilization with magnificent cities and riches. The kingdom was created and ruled by Poseidon, the god of the sea.

After many years of prosperous life under Poseidon's laws, trouble brewed in Atlantis. Its people became proud and greedy, and forgot the laws that kept the civilization running smoothly. So, the story goes, the gods punished Atlantis. A great earthquake shook the whole continent, bringing on floods and storms. The whole island sank into the sea.

This story incites the imagination. Many wonder if Atlantis was real or just another Greek myth. There are those who believe it did exist and some who think the story has no basis in fact. Some think the great city still lies beneath the ocean, inhabited by sea creatures such as mermaids and mermen. Many expeditions have tried to discover the remains of the island. There are even some predictions that the continent will again rise from the sea.

Could a real place have inspired Plato's imagination? Some scientists and scholars think so. The Aegean island of Thira was destroyed in 1470 BC by a volcanic eruption. This disaster wiped out a large portion of the Minoan civilization.
Read:
1. inspires
2. Poseidon
3. an earthquake that generated floods and storms
4. Answers will vary.